Happy Thanksgiving,
Team Charles!

Lookin forward to shareing

a meal soon.

love,

Brian & Francie

Savor Nantucket

Savor Nantucket

CREATIVELY CASUAL CUISINE

PHOTOGRAPHY BY JEFFREY ALLEN

COLLECTED RECIPES FROM THE PARISHIONERS AND FRIENDS OF THE
CHURCH OF ST. MARY—OUR LADY OF THE ISLE

Savor Nantucket
CREATIVELY CASUAL CUISINE

COLLECTED RECIPES FROM THE PARISHIONERS AND FRIENDS
OF THE CHURCH ST. MARY—OUR LADY OF THE ISLE

PUBLISHED BY ST. MARY—OUR LADY OF THE ISLE CATHOLIC CHURCH, NANTUCKET, MASSACHUSETTS

COPYRIGHT ©2008
ST. MARY—OUR LADY OF THE ISLE
3 FEDERAL STREET
P.O. BOX 1168
NANTUCKET, MA 02554

To order, visit our website: www.stmarysnantucket.org / cookbook

PHOTOGRAPHY © JEFFREY ALLEN PHOTOGRAPHY
EDITED AND DESIGNED BY KATHLEEN HAY DESIGNS
COPY EDITED BY ELIZABETH OLDHAM

NANTUCKET BASKET CHINA DESIGNED BY GEO. P. DAVIS FOR WEDGWOOD

This cookbook is a collection of favorite recipes, which are not necessarily original; most have been tested for
accuracy, but we cannot be held responsible for errors or omissions. We regret that we were unable to include many of the recipes
submitted due to similarity or lack of space.

Library of Congress Control Number:
ISBN: 978-0-615-18533-0

PRINTED BY HANOVER PRINTING CO., HANOVER, NEW HAMPSHIRE

MANUFACTURED IN THE UNITED STATES OF AMERICA
FIRST EDITION, 2008

St. Mary–Our Lady of the Isle

Nantucket Island

THE HISTORY OF ST. MARY—OUR LADY OF THE ISLE

For more than a hundred years, the Catholic people of Nantucket have followed their faith in the parish church on Federal Street, which has remained virtually unchanged since it was built. It was a Saturday afternoon in the spring of 1849 when the New Bedford packet boat arrived in Nantucket. A small group of Nantucketers were at the dock to meet a passenger, Father Thomas McNulty of New Bedford. He was the first Roman Catholic priest ever known to have conducted a religious service on Nantucket.

Father McNulty arrived to find three hundred Catholics living on the island, which then had a population of 8,800 people. The Roman Catholic Church in New England considered Nantucket to be mission territory, nominally under the supervision of the New Bedford parish but having neither a church building nor a resident clergy. The few Catholics on the island at that time were mostly Irish immigrants who had fled the potato famine, and who were obliged to conduct their own prayer services with neither clergy nor sacraments. The first Mass was celebrated in the spring of 1849 by Father McNulty in the old Town Hall, which stood on Main Street. Father McNulty retired in 1858.

Father Henry Henniss succeeded Father McNulty. During the decade of the 1850s, Nantucket's population declined from 8,880 to 6,094, as the island suffered economic losses following the decline of the whaling industry, the Great Fire of 1846, and the departure of many people for California after gold was discovered. Despite the meager finances of his flock, Father Henniss had the vision to find a permanent place of worship for the parish. Whether by good fortune or divine guidance, he was able to purchase a large hall centrally located in downtown Nantucket—Harmony Hall. This hall was erected at Federal and Cambridge Streets after the Great Fire, and had been used for public events. By 1880, the growth of Nantucket as a summer resort brought a demand for construction workers. The local Catholic population expanded to the point where the attendance at the summer Masses was doubled; the need for a permanent parish became apparent.

In 1896, Father Cornelius McSweeney was given permission by Bishop Harkins to build a church in Nantucket. Harmony Hall was to be auctioned off. It sold to John Roberts for $145, with the condition that he remove the structure in twenty-one days. The site, which included several other structures, was cleared within a month. Construction began January 1, 1897, and was completed in eight months. The new church, called the Church of St. Mary—Our Lady of the Isle, was complete, and stands—without change in form—a hundred years later.

So, in the course of time, the little Church of St. Mary has become a source of pride for Nantucket's Catholic community. Starting with a humble flock of three hundred immigrants, it has grown to minister to a year-round Catholic population of around 2,500. The parish grows fivefold in the summer, with six Masses held each weekend. St. Mary's continues to provide religious education for hundreds of Nantucket children every year, and sends many on to higher education. Most important, the doors of the church are open every day—summer and winter, fall and spring—accepting all who might find solace at this shrine in the sea: St. Mary—Our Lady of the Isle.

— Bob Mooney

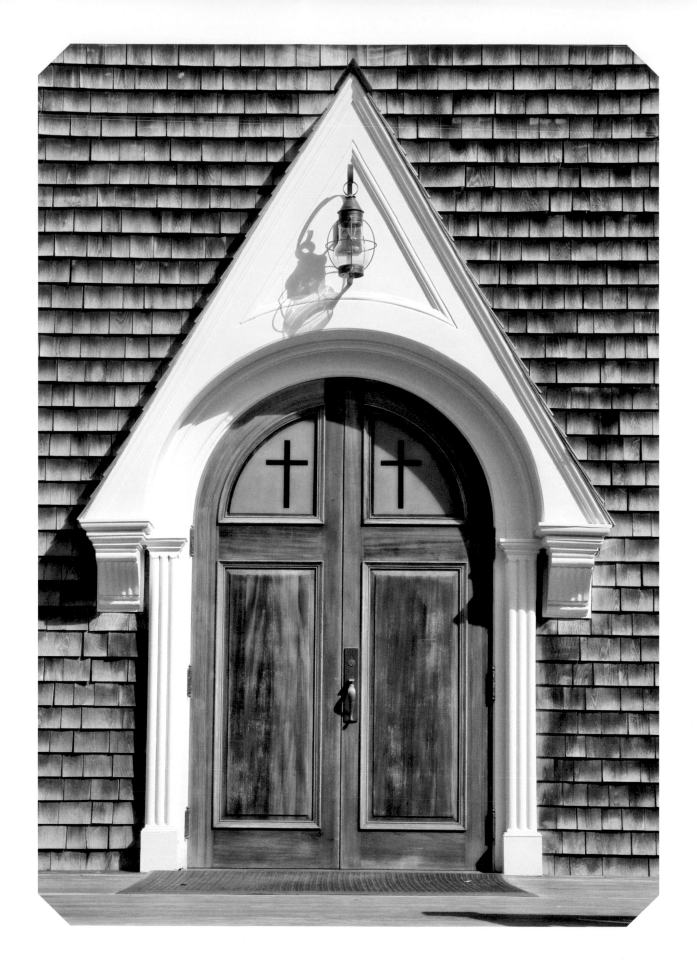

Dedication

This book is dedicated to Father Paul Caron, who served as pastor of St. Mary's from 2000 to 2007.

Father Paul's love for Nantucket and the St. Mary's parish family was apparent from the day he stepped onto the shores of the Grey Lady. During his seven years as pastor, he served the entire Nantucket community unselfishly, as both a spiritual leader and a friend.

Born and raised in Taunton, Massachusetts, Father Paul graduated from college with a degree in biology. He had plans to pursue a career in medicine, but instead he became an educator— teaching in both public and parochial schools for six years. In 1978, he entered the seminary. He comments, "I had a nagging and continuous feeling to answer the call to the priesthood. The 'phone kept ringing,' but I didn't answer it for years. I wanted to become a diocesan priest."

After graduating from St. John Seminary in Brighton, Massachusetts, he had multiple diocesan assignments. In 2000, Father Paul was transferred to Nantucket where he remained parish priest at St. Mary—Our Lady of the Isle for seven years.

Father Paul could often be seen dining at one of our many local restaurants. His love for food ranged from simple island fare to gourmet cuisine. He enthusiastically shared recipes with island residents, as well as many restaurant owners.

"I believe that if you embrace something, it will embrace you in return. You can actually fall in love with a parish—the people. That is what happened to me on Nantucket, and specifically at St. Mary's. I fell in love."

Father, we dedicate this cookbook to you, with our love.

Cookbook Committee

CHAIR
Jo-Ann Winn

RECIPE TEXT
John McGuinn
Rosanne McGuinn
Laurie Paterson
Kate O'Connor
Nonie Slavitz
Jo-Ann Winn

SPECIAL EVENTS COORDINATOR
Kate O'Connor

RECIPE WEBSITE
Miki Lovett

MARKETING AND DISTRIBUTION
Mary Malavase

TREASURER/FINANCE
Carol Marks

GRAPHIC DESIGN, EDITING AND LAYOUT
Kathleen Hay

PHOTOGRAPHY
Jeffrey Allen

COPY EDITOR
Elizabeth Oldham

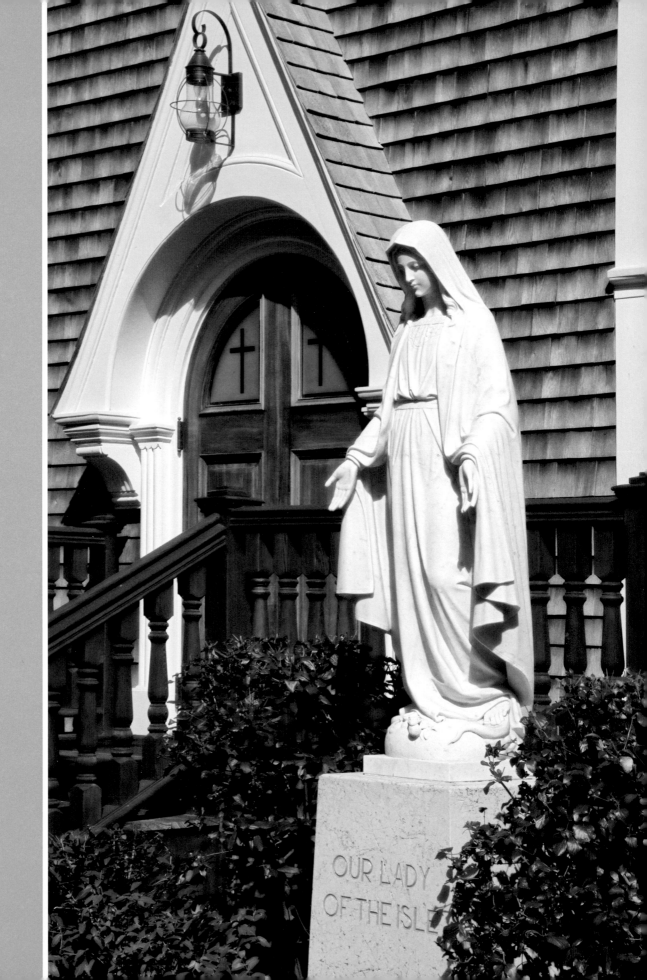

$\mathcal{C}$ontents

Savor
THE BEGINNINGS

APPETIZERS AND NIBBLES

ANTIPASTO JUMBLE

ANTIPASTO
1 pint (2 cups) grape tomatoes
1 cup fresh baby carrots
1 cup pitted Kalamata olives
6 oz. string cheese, cut into ½-inch chunks (about 1 cup)
1 jar (7 oz.) stuffed large Queen green olives (about 1 cup), drained
1 jar (6 oz.) Green Giant® whole mushrooms, drained

MARINADE
1/4 cup refrigerated basil pesto
1/4 cup Italian dressing
1 tsp. grated orange peel
1/2 tsp. crushed red pepper flakes

In a large glass bowl, mix all antipasto ingredients.

In a small bowl, mix all marinade ingredients until well blended. Pour marinade over antipasto; toss well. Refrigerate at least 1 hour or until serving time.

CHEESE STICKS

1 loaf unsliced dry white bread
3 oz. cream cheese, softened
12 oz. sharp Cheddar cheese, shredded (3 cups)
1/2 cup (1 stick) butter or margarine
2 egg whites, stiffly beaten

Trim the crusts from the bread. Cut the bread into 1½-inch-long sticks. Melt the cream cheese, Cheddar cheese, and butter in a double boiler over hot water until of a rarebit consistency. Remove from the heat to cool. Fold in the stiffly beaten egg whites. Dip the bread sticks into the mixture, coating all sides. Arrange on a baking sheet and freeze. Store the frozen cheese sticks in seal-able plastic freezer bags until ready to serve. To serve, arrange the frozen cheese sticks on a baking sheet. Bake at 400 degrees for 10 to 15 minutes or until golden brown. Yield: 8–10 servings

OLIVE TAPENADE

1 1/2 cups chopped pimento-stuffed green olives
1 tbsp. garlic, finely chopped
1/3 cup red onion, finely chopped
1 large red bell pepper, finely chopped
1/2 cup toasted pine nuts, chopped
1/4 cup grated Parmesan cheese
6 tbsp. Italian salad dressing

Process the green olives, garlic, onion, bell pepper, pine nuts, and cheese in a food processor until smooth. Add the salad dressing and mix well. Serve with baguette slices or crackers. Yield: 10 servings

BLUEFISH PATÉ

2 tsp. onion, chopped
8 oz. smoked bluefish, skinned
8 oz. sweet butter, room temp.
5 oz. cream cheese, room temp.
2 1/2 tsp. anchovy paste
2 1/2 tsp. cognac
1/2 tsp. Worcestershire sauce
Juice of half a lemon

In an electric blender or food processor blend, in order, onion, cut up bluefish, anchovy paste, cream cheese, butter, lemon juice, cognac, and Worcestershire sauce.

The recipe was developed by Rene Beach for the first Seafest in 1979. It is the original and best bluefish paté recipe we know.

CHIVE-PINE NUT DIP
(a different twist on onion dip)

1 bunch chives
1/4 cup olive oil
1/4 tsp. salt
1 (8-oz.) pkg. cream cheese, room temperature
1 container mascarpone cheese, room temperature
1/2 cup pine nuts

Toast pine nuts in frying pan, 3 minutes. Chop roughly and set aside.

In a small food processor, blend olive oil, half of the chives, and the salt. Press mixture through a strainer into a small bowl. It will be the consistency of oil.

In a large mixing bowl, add cream cheese, mascarpone cheese, and chive oil. Add the other half of the chives, minced, and the chopped pine nuts. Add additional salt and freshly ground pepper to taste. Serve with potato chips or crackers. Makes 2 cups.

BAKED STUFFED MUSHROOMS

1 pkg. stuffing mushrooms
1/2 lb. crabmeat, chopped
1/2 lb. lobster meat, chopped
1/2 lb. cream cheese (16 oz. package)
3/4 cup garlic croutons, finely crushed
1 stick of butter, melted
1 stick of butter
1 pkg. shredded mozzarella cheese

In a saucepan melt the cream cheese, add the croutons and melted butter and mix well. If mixture is too dry add more melted butter. Add the crabmeat and lobster. Fill the mushroom caps with the mixture. Place in a large pan with 2" sides. Cut up another stick of butter and place in the pan. Top each filled mushroom cap with mozzarella cheese. Bake at 350 degrees for 25–30 minutes.

CUCUMBER-DILL STUFFED CHERRY TOMATOES

24 cherry tomatoes
1 pkg. (3 oz.) cream cheese, softened
2 tbsp. mayonnaise or salad dressing
1/4 cup seeded cucumber, finely chopped
1 tbsp. green onions, finely chopped
2 tsp. chopped fresh or 1/4 tsp. dried dill weed

Remove stems from tomatoes. To level bottoms of tomatoes, cut thin slice from bottom of each. Starting at stem end and using small spoon or melon baller, carefully hollow out each tomato, leaving 1/8-inch shell. Invert tomato shells onto paper towels to drain.

CRAB SPREAD

2 (7-oz.) cans crabmeat
1 envelope unflavored gelatin
1 (10-oz.) can tomato soup
8 oz. cream cheese, softened
1 cup mayonnaise
1/2 cup chopped scallions
1/2 cup chopped celery
10 to 20 drops of Tabasco sauce

Flake and drain the crabmeat, reserving 1/4 cup of the liquid. Soften the gelatin in the reserved liquid in a bowl. Heat the soup and cream cheese in a double boiler until the cream cheese melts, whisking until smooth. Remove from the heat. Add the gelatin mixture and whisk until dissolved. Add the mayonnaise, scallions, celery, and Tabasco sauce and mix well. Spoon into an oiled mold. Chill, covered, for 6 to 8 hours or until firm. Unmold onto a serving plate. Serve with crackers. Yield: 20 servings

RADICCHIO WITH WILD MUSHROOMS AND PARSLEY

1 lb. fresh wild mushrooms (chanterelles, pleurottes, shiitake, porcini), cleaned
6 tbsp. olive oil
Salt and freshly ground pepper to taste
6 tbsp. chopped fresh parsley
1/2 cup heavy cream
40 small radicchio leaves (about 6 small heads)

Cut the mushrooms into small pieces approximately 1/2 inch square. Sauté in olive oil for 2 to 3 minutes. Season with salt and pepper. Add parsley and cream and bring to a simmer. Remove from heat. Spoon onto small radicchio leaves and serve immediately. Yield: 40 hors d'oeuvres

MINIATURE BLINI

2 cups small-curd cottage cheese
1 tbsp. sour cream
1 tsp. vanilla extract
1/2 tsp. sugar
3 tbsp. butter, melted
3 eggs
1/2 cup baking mix (such as Bisquick®)

Process the cottage cheese, sour cream, vanilla, sugar and butter in a food processor until well mixed. Add the eggs one at a time, processing constantly after each addition. Add the baking mix and mix well. Pour into greased miniature muffin cups, filling each cup 3/4 full. Bake at 350 degrees for 20 to 25 minutes or until golden brown. Remove the muffin cups to cool. Serve with a dollop of sour cream and top with gold or black caviar. Yield: 8–10 servings

Note: Blini may be frozen after baking and thawed before adding the toppings and serving.

PHYLLO AND SPINACH CUPS

1 pkg. frozen phyllo dough, thawed
1/4 cup butter, melted
1 (10-oz.) package frozen chopped spinach, thawed
1/3 cup onion, minced
3 tbsp. butter
1/4 lb. Parmesan cheese
2 eggs, beaten
3/4 cup mozzarella cheese, grated
2 tsp. bread crumbs
1/4 tsp. salt
1/4 tsp. pepper
1/4 tsp. ground nutmeg

Cut phyllo dough into 3" squares. Brush with melted butter. Stack four buttered squares and mold into mini muffin tins. Bake at 450 degrees for 5 minutes, until light brown and holds shape when removed from tin. Set aside on a cookie sheet. Yield: 3 dozen.

For filling: Sauté onion in butter until translucent. Add spinach. Cook 5 minutes and cool. Add Parmesan cheese, eggs, bread crumbs, mozzarella cheese, salt, pepper, and nutmeg. Mix well. Fill phyllo cups with spinach mixture. Bake 10–15 minutes at 450 degrees or until cheese is bubbly and phyllo cups are golden brown. Serve hot. Yield: 36 servings

Savor THE BEGINNINGS
APPETIZERS AND NIBBLES

MUSHROOMS ROCKEFELLER

18 large fresh button mushrooms (about 1 pound)
2 slices of bacon
1/2 cup chopped onion
1 (10-oz.) pkg. frozen chopped spinach, thawed and squeezed dry
1 tbsp. lemon juice
1 tsp. grated lemon peel
1/2 jar (2 oz.) chopped pimentos, drained
Lemon slices and lemon peel for garnish

Lightly spray 13x9-inch baking dish with nonstick cooking spray. Preheat
oven to 375 degrees. Brush dirt from mushrooms; clean by wiping
mushrooms with damp paper towel Pull entire stem out of each
mushroom cap; reserve.

Cut thin slice from base of each stem; discard. Chop remaining portions
of stems.

Cook bacon in medium skillet over medium heat until crisp. Remove
bacon with tongs to paper towel; set aside. Add mushroom stems
and onion to hot drippings in skillet. Cook and stir till onion is soft. Add
spinach, lemon juice, lemon peel, and pimento; blend well. Stuff
mushroom caps with spinach mixture; place in single layer in
prepared baking dish. Crumble reserved bacon and sprinkle on top
of mushrooms. Bake 15 minutes or until heated through. Garnish, if
desired. Serve immediately. Yield: 18 mushrooms

SKEWERED TORTELLINI WITH PARMESAN LEMON DIP

1 1/2 lb. tortellini
Several heads of garlic

DIP
1 cup crème fraîche
1/4 cup grated Parmesan cheese
Juice of 2 lemons
Grated zest of 2 lemons
3 cloves roasted garlic
olive oil

Bring a large kettle of lightly salted water to a boil and cook the tortellini until just tender. Drain the pasta and sprinkle with some olive oil to prevent sticking. Roast several heads of garlic, lightly sprinkled with olive oil, for about 1 hour, or until golden brown and soft. Separate the cloves and store in a container filled with olive oil. Combine all the ingredients for the dip in a small mixing bowl. Set aside until ready to use. Put 2 warm tortellini on small, 6-inch skewers and serve immediately with dip. Yield: 40 skewers

KAHLÚA BAKED BRIE

1/4 cup packed dark brown sugar
1/4 cup Kahlúa
1 1/4 cups chopped roasted pecans
1 (14-oz.) miniature wheel Brie cheese

Bring the brown sugar and Kahlúa to a boil in a small saucepan over medium heat and reduce the heat. Cook for 5 minutes, stirring occasionally. Remove from the heat and stir in the pecans.

Remove the rind from the cheese using a sharp knife. Arrange in a 9-inch glass pie plate or similar microwave-safe dish. Pour the Kahlúa mixture over the cheese. Microwave on high for 1 1/2 to 2 minutes or until cheese softens. Watch carefully so the cheese will not overheat and melt. Serve with toasted French bread rounds or sliced fruit. Yield: 8 servings

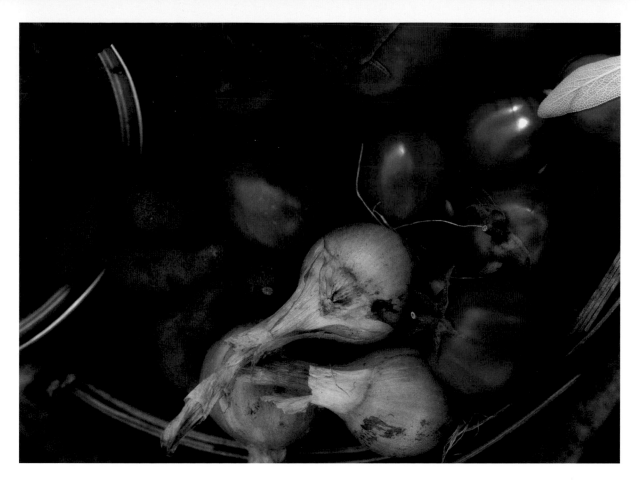

RED POTATOES WITH SOUR CREAM AND CAVIAR

Choose the smallest, most blemish-free, red-skinned potatoes. Allow 2 to 3 potatoes per person. Wash the potatoes and either boil gently until tender or bake in a 350 degree oven until tender, about 30 minutes.

To serve, cut the potatoes in half and place cut-side down on trays. With a melon-ball scoop, spoon out some of the top to create a small cavity. Fill with a dollop of sour cream and top with red caviar (salmon), black caviar (Sevruga or Osetra), or golden caviar (whitefish).

Topping variations:
Sautéed onion
Crumbled crisp bacon
Sour cream and fresh herbs
Chopped ham
Chopped scallions
Grated cheese
Chopped walnuts
Coarse salt, freshly ground pepper, and melted butter

ORANGE-GINGER SHRIMP SNACKS

1/2 cup vegetable oil
1/4 cup vinegar
1/4 cup frozen orange juice concentrate, thawed
1 tbsp. chopped red onion
2 tsp. grated ginger root
3/4 tsp. crushed red pepper flakes
1 lb. uncooked medium shrimp, deveined and peeled
5 bamboo skewers (12 inch)

In a blender, place all ingredients except shrimp and skewers; process until well blended. In large resealable food-storage plastic bag, place shrimp. Pour oil mixture over shrimp; let stand at room temperature 15 minutes to marinate. Soak bamboo skewers in water while shrimp are marinating.

Drain shrimp, discarding marinade. Thread shrimp onto bamboo skewers; place on ungreased cookie sheet. Broil 6 inches from heat 3 to 5 minutes, turning once, until shrimp turn pink. With kitchen scissors, cut each skewer into 3 pieces.
Yield: 15 servings

STUFFED SCAMPI

1 clove garlic, chopped
1/4 cup fresh bread crumbs
1/4 cup grated Parmesan cheese
1/4 cup olive oil
1 1/2 lb. (24 to 30) large shrimp, peeled and de veined (tail intact)
Lemon juice
Black pepper

Preheat the broiler.

Mix together garlic, bread crumbs, cheese, and oil in a bowl. Stuff each shrimp with the mixture and put them on a cookie sheet. Place the sheet on the highest oven rack and broil the shrimp about 2 minutes per side.

The stuffed shrimp can be served hot, at room temperature, or chilled, with freshly squeezed lemon juice and ground pepper to taste. Yield: 6–8 servings

Savor THE BEGINNINGS
APPETIZERS AND NIBBLES

"SUMMERWINNS" LOBSTER ENDIVE

1 cup crème fraîche
1/2 tsp. finely grated fresh lemon zest
1/2 tsp. finely grated fresh lime zest
1/2 tsp. finely grated orange zest
1 tsp. fresh lemon juice
1 tsp. fresh lime juice
1 tsp. fresh orange juice
1 tsp. fresh chopped tarragon leaves
2 Belgian endives
1 1/2 lb. cooked lobster meat
1 bunch fresh chives

In a bowl stir together crème fraîche, zests, juices, tarragon, and salt and pepper to taste. Chill sauce, covered, for one hour to blend flavors.

Just before serving, coarsely chop lobster. In another bowl, stir lobster together with 3/4 cup sauce. Separate endive leaves. Fill each leaf with lobster mixture. Garnish with fresh minced chives.

Note: Crème fraîche can be purchased already prepared.

BAY SCALLOP PUFFS

1 1/2 tbsp. unsalted butter
1/2 lb. bay scallops, quartered
1/2 tsp. finely minced lemon zest
2 cloves garlic, minced
1 1/2 tbsp. chopped fresh dill
1 cup Gruyère (or Swiss) cheese, grated
1 cup mayonnaise
1/4 tsp. freshly ground pepper
72 (one-inch) white bread rounds (or triangles), lightly toasted
1/4 tsp. paprika
Lemon slices and fresh dill for garnish

Melt butter in a sauté pan. Add scallops, lemon zest, and garlic. Cook
for 2–3 minutes, stirring constantly until scallops are just barely
cooked. Add dill and cook 20 seconds longer. Let cool.

Add cheese, mayonnaise, and pepper to scallop mixture and combine
well. Refrigerate in covered bowl until ready to prepare, but no longer
than a week.

Preheat broiler. Place toast rounds on baking sheets and top each
round with scallop mixture. Sprinkle lightly with paprika, Broil puffs for
2–3 minutes until puffs are golden. Serve hot. Yield: 20–25

CLAMS CASINO

16–20 littleneck clams, opened
1/4 cup onion, finely chopped
1/2 cup seasoned bread crumbs
1/2-1 lb. Cheddar cheese, sliced
6–8 strips of bacon
1/4 cup Parmesan cheese, grated
1/2 tsp. oregano
1/2 tsp. basil
1/2 tsp. pepper

Place clams in half-shell onto a broiler pan. Sprinkle with onion, oregano, basil, and pepper. Follow each with bread crumbs. Top each with a square of cheese. Cut bacon into 1 1/2–2 inch squares and top each clam. Finally, sprinkle with Parmesan cheese. Broil under high heat until bacon is done, 5–7 minutes.

GARLIC-STUFFED CLAMS

1/2 cup (1 stick) unsalted butter
6 cloves garlic, minced
1/2 cup chopped fresh parsley
1/4 cup packed fresh basil leaves, cut into fine shreds
24 Littleneck clams, shucked and meat finely chopped
    (save shells and scrub to remove any grit), or 2 (8-oz.)
    cans chopped clams, drained
2 cups fresh French bread crumbs
1 cup freshly grated Parmesan cheese

In a medium-sized skillet over low heat, melt the butter. Add the garlic and cook until the butter is infused with the flavor of the garlic, about 5 minutes. Don't allow the garlic or butter to turn color. Stir in the parsley and basil and set aside.

In a medium-sized bowl, stir together the clams, bread crumbs, and Parmesan cheese. Dribble in about half the butter mixture, until the crumbs appear moist but not soggy. Stuff the reserved clamshells or oven-proof, store-bought shells with the mixture. Transfer to a baking sheet and drizzle each clam with a bit of the remaining garlic butter.

At this point, you can cover and refrigerate for up to 2 days.

Preheat the oven to 350 degrees. Bake the clams until heated through or when the tops begin to turn golden brown, 15 to 20 minutes. Transfer to a platter and serve warm or at room temperature.

Serves 10–12

DEVILED EGGS WITH SHRIMP

1/3 to 1/2 cup chopped cooked shrimp
2 tbsp. fresh lemon or lime juice
8 large eggs
1/4 tsp. dry mustard
3 tbsp. mayonnaise
1/2 tsp. cider vinegar
Bottled horseradish
Salt
Freshly ground pepper
Chopped fresh chives or parsley

Put shrimp in a glass bowl and toss with lemon juice. Set aside. Place the eggs in a medium saucepan, cover with water, and bring to a boil. Let boil for about 30 seconds. Remove from the heat and let sit for 15 minutes. Run the eggs under cold water, peel, and halve.

Place the cooked yolks in a bowl and mash them with the mustard, mayonnaise, cider vinegar, and horseradish using a fork. Add salt and pepper to taste. Drain the shrimp and mix them with the egg yolks. You may need to add additional mayonnaise. Stuff the whites, garnish with chopped chives or parsley leaves, cover with plastic wrap, and refrigerate.

Serves 4

Savor THE BEGINNINGS
APPETIZERS AND NIBBLES

POLENTA WITH SUN-DRIED TOMATO SALSA

POLENTA:
2 3/4 cups water
3/4 teaspoon kosher salt
1/2 cup polenta
1/2 heavy cream
1/2 cup freshly grated Parmesan cheese

SALSA:
1 1/4 cup oil-packed sun-dried tomatoes, drained and julienned
3 tbsp. chopped fresh basil
1 tbsp. balsamic vinegar
3/4 tsp. minced garlic

Lightly oil an 8-by-8-by-2½-inch glass baking dish. Bring the water and salt to a boil in a heavy, medium saucepan over medium-high heat. Whisk in the polenta. Reduce the heat and simmer for about 10 minutes. Remove from the heat and whisk in the Parmesan cheese. Pour the polenta mixture into the prepared baking dish and spread evenly into the dish using a plastic spatula. Refrigerate until chilled. Mix the tomatoes, basil, vinegar, and garlic together in a small bowl.

To assemble: Preheat the oven to 300 degrees. Trim the edges of the polenta and cut into 36 squares. Top each square with 1/2 teaspoon of the salsa. Place on a foil- or parchment paper-lined baking sheet. Bake until slightly warm, 8 to 10 minutes. Serve warm. Yield: 36 polenta squares

TORTILLA WRAPS

6 oz. cream cheese at room temperature
4 oz. mild chevre cheese (Montrachet)
1 clove garlic, minced
3 scallions, trimmed and minced
1 can (4 oz.) green chilis
6 sun-dried tomatoes packed in oil, drained but reserve oil, thinly sliced
1/3 cup pitted black olives, minced
4 oz. Monterey Jack cheese, shredded
1 cup cooked chicken meat, finely diced
3 tbsp. cilantro, minced
2 tsp. chili powder
Cayenne pepper to taste
14 large (10-inch) flour tortillas

Beat the cream cheese and chevre together in a mixing bowl until smooth. Beat in all the remaining ingredients (except tortillas and reserved sun-dried oil). Spread one tortilla with a generous 2 tbsp. of the cheese mixture. Roll up the tortilla, jelly-roll style, and wrap in plastic wrap. Repeat the process with the remaining cheese mixture, and refrigerate for two hours.

Preheat oven to 400 degrees.

Cut each tortilla roll into 1/2 inch slices and place cut sides up on nonstick cookie sheet. Brush each slice with the sun-dried tomato oil. Bake until browned, 12 to15 minutes.

ARTICHOKE NIBBLES

1 small onion, chopped
1 clove garlic, minced
1 tsp. vegetable oil
2 (6-oz.) jars marinated artichoke hearts, drained and chopped
4 eggs
2 tbsp. fresh Italian parsley, minced
1/4 tsp. salt
1/8 tsp. pepper
1/8 tsp. oregano
1/8 tsp. hot pepper sauce
2 cups (8 oz.) Cheddar cheese, shredded
1/3 cup Saltines, crushed (about 10)

In a small skillet, sauté onion and garlic in oil until tender. Stir in artichokes. Remove from the heat and set aside. In a large bowl, whisk the eggs, parsley, salt, pepper, oregano, and hot pepper sauce. Stir in cheese, cracker crumbs, and artichoke mixture.

Pour into a greased 11x17x2-inch baking dish. Bake uncovered at 325 degrees for 25 to 30 minutes, or until a knife inserted in the center comes out clean. Cool 10 to 15 minutes before cutting into squares. Serve warm.

Savor
THE DAWN

BREAKFAST, BREADS, AND BRUNCH

EGGS DIVAN

1 pkg. frozen broccoli spears
6 hard-cooked eggs
1 small can deviled ham
1/4 tsp. Worcestershire sauce
1/2 tsp. salt
1/2 tsp. dry mustard
1 tbsp. milk

SAUCE:
2 tbsp. flour
1 1/2 tbsp. butter, melted
1/2 tsp. dry mustard
1/2 tsp. salt
1 cup milk
1 cup grated sharp cheese
buttered bread crumbs

Cook broccoli as directed on package. Slice eggs lengthwise and remove yolks. Mash yolks and add deviled ham, Worcestershire sauce, onion, salt, dry mustard, and milk. Mix well and fill egg whites. Place broccoli in a buttered 8x8-inch dish. Place eggs on top.

Blend flour, butter, and seasonings. Add milk and cheese. Heat until thick and smooth, stirring constantly. Pour over eggs and top with bread crumbs. Bake at 350 degrees for 25 minutes. Serves 4–5

OATMEAL RAISIN SCONES

3 cups flour
1/2 cup brown sugar
1 1/4 tsp. baking powder
3/4 tsp. baking soda
3/4 tsp. salt
6 oz. chilled butter
2 1/4 cup rolled oats
3/4 cup raisins
1 1/2 cups buttermilk

In a food processor, combine the flour, sugar, baking powder, baking soda, and salt. Mix. Add butter and pulse until butter is pea-sized. Turn into a large bowl. Add the oats, raisins, and buttermilk. Scoop into parchment-lined pans. Bake at 375 degrees for 20 minutes.

MORNING GLORY MUFFINS

by Geo. Davis and Bruce Dilts, original owners of the Morning Glory Café

4 cups all-purpose flour
2 1/2 cups sugar
4 tsp. baking soda
4 tsp. cinnamon
1 tsp. salt
Pinch of nutmeg
4 cups grated carrot

1 cup raisins, plumped in bourbon
1 cup chopped pecans
1 cup sweetened shredded coconut
2 apples, peeled, cored, and grated
6 large eggs
2 cups vegetable oil
4 tsp. vanilla

In a large bowl, sift together the flour, sugar, baking soda, cinnamon, salt and nutmeg. Stir in grated carrot, raisins, chopped pecans, coconut, and apples.

In a bowl, beat the eggs with the oil and vanilla. Stir the egg mixture into the flour mixture until the batter is just combined. Spoon the batter into well-buttered 1/2-cup muffin tins, filling them to the top. Bake the muffins in a preheated, 350-degree oven for 35 minutes or until the muffins are springy to the touch. Let the muffins cool in the tins on a rack for 5 minutes. Turn them out onto the rack and let them cool completely. Yield: 30 muffins

SUNDAY MORNING CRÊPES

1 cup flour
1 tbsp. sugar
1/4 tsp. salt
1 cup milk
1/3 cup water
3 eggs
3 tbsp. unsalted butter, melted

Combine flour, sugar, and salt in food processor. With motor running add milk, water, eggs, and butter. Process until smooth. Heat a heavy 7-inch, nonstick skillet until hot. Pour in 3 to 4 tablespoons batter, then quickly tilt pan to spread evenly, forming a crêpe. Cook 30 to 45 seconds, until lightly browned. Turn for another 15 seconds on the other side. Repeat, using all the batter.

As you finish the crêpes, stack between sheets of wax paper to prevent sticking. When all crêpes are cooked, serve with powdered sugar, fresh berries, or maple syrup.

PRALINE BRUNCH TOAST

8 eggs
1 1/2 cups half-and-half
1 tbsp. brown sugar
2 tsp. vanilla extract
8 thick slices sourdough bread
1/2 cup (1 stick) butter
3/4 cup packed brown sugar
1/2 cup maple syrup
3/4 cup chopped pecans

Beat the eggs and half-and-half in a small bowl. Whisk in the brown sugar and vanilla. Pour 1/2 the egg mixture into a 9x13-inch baking dish. Arrange the bread slices in the dish, trimming the crusts to fit if necessary. Pour the remaining egg mixture over the bread. Chill, covered, for several hours or overnight.

Melt the butter in another 9x13-inch baking dish. Stir in 3/4 cup brown sugar and the syrup. Sprinkle the pecans over the bottom. Place the egg-soaked bread slices carefully on top of the pecans with a spatula. Pour the remaining egg mixture over the bread. Bake at 350 degrees for 30 to 35 minutes or until the bread is light brown and puffed. To serve, invert the toast onto plates and spoon pecans from the bottom of the dish over the toast.

DUTCH BABIES

4 medium apples, peeled and sliced
6 tbsp. butter
6 eggs, beaten
1 cup milk
1 cup all-purpose flour
Dash of salt
4 to 6 tbsp. butter
Confectioners' sugar

Sauté the apples in 6 tablespoons butter in a skillet until tender. Beat the eggs, milk, flour, and salt in a bowl. Melt 4 to 6 tablespoons butter in a cast-iron skillet. Add the egg mixture. Bake at 400 degrees for 20 minutes. Remove from the oven and sprinkle with confectioners' sugar. Spoon the sautéed apples into the middle. Yield: 6 servings

Note: You may serve with syrup and lemon wedges instead of the sautéed apples.

DATE AND NUT BREAD

2 cups dates, cut up
1 1/2 cups white sugar
2 tbsp. shortening
1 1/2 cups boiling water
1 egg
3 cups flour
2 tsp. baking soda
1/2 tsp. salt
2 tsp. vanilla
1 cup chopped nuts

Mix the first four ingredients. Cool to lukewarm. Add remaining ingredients and mix well. Preheat oven to 325 degrees. Bake in greased and floured loaf pans for 1 hour. If using small loaf pans, check for doneness in about 50 minutes.

MARY'S SOUR CREAM BREAD

1/2 lb. (2 sticks) butter, softened,
2 cups sugar
4 eggs
2 tsp. vanilla
4 cups flour
2 tsp. baking powder
1 pint sour cream
2 tsp. baking soda

TOPPING
1/2 cup chopped walnuts or pecans
1 cup sugar
2 tsp. cinnamon

In a large bowl, cream together butter, sugar, eggs, and vanilla. Sift together flour, baking powder, and baking soda. Add sour cream and flour mixture to butter mixture. Blend until just moistened. Mix topping in separate bowl.

Grease and flour two 8x5-inch bread pans. Divide batter into bread pans, making 3 layers with topping mixture in between each layer and on top. Bake in preheated 350 degree oven for 50 minutes.

CRANBERRY-STRAWBERRY JAM

2 cups fresh whole cranberries
2 (10 oz.) pkgs. frozen strawberries in quick-thaw pouch
5 1/2 cups sugar
1 pouch Certo liquid pectin

Mix fruit with sugar in a large pot. Bring to a full, rolling boil over medium-high heat until cranberries start to pop open. Use a potato masher to crush berries. Bring to a full, rolling boil again, stirring constantly for 4 minutes. Remove from the heat and stir in Certo liquid pectin. Return to heat and boil for one minute. Remove from heat. Stir with a metal spoon and skim foam for 5 minutes. Cool slightly to prevent fruit from floating to the top of the jam. Pour immediately into a warm sterilized jars, filling to within 1/4 inch of the rim. Seal while hot with paraffin and jar lids. Let stand at room temperature until set.

NANTUCKET BEACH PLUM JELLY

7 cups beach plums, cooked to 4 cups of juice
6 1/2 cups sugar
1 pouch Certo liquid pectin

Pick the beach plums in early September when ripe to equal 7 cups of berries. Cook in a large pot with about 3/4 cup of water to prevent beach plums from sticking to the bottom of the pot. Cook for 15 to 20 minutes at medium heat until beach plums soften and start to pop. Mash with a potato masher to release all the juice. Strain through a jelly bag or colander lined with cheese cloth.

Measure 4 cups of juice and mix with 6 1/2 cups sugar in a large pot. Bring to a full, rolling boil over medium-high heat until jelly coats the back of a spoon in a thick stream. Boil 3 to 5 minutes, stirring constantly. Remove from the heat. Immediately stir in one pouch of Certo liquid pectin.* Stir with a metal spoon and skim foam for 5 minutes. Pour immediately into warm sterilized jars, filling to within 1/4 inch of rim. Seal while hot with paraffin and jar lids. Let stand at room temperature until set.

*If beach plums are not fully ripe, it might be necessary to add additional pectin.

Savor THE DAWN
BREAKFAST, BREADS, AND BRUNCH

LEMON TEA BREAD

1 cup sugar
5 tbsp. butter
2 eggs
Grated rind of 1 lemon
1/2 cup milk
1/2 tsp. salt
1 1/2 cups flour
1 tsp. flour
1 tsp. baking powder
1/2 cup nuts, finely chopped, optional

GLAZE:
Juice of 1 lemon
1/2 cup sugar

Blend butter and sugar until creamy. Beat in the eggs. Add milk and mix well. Sift dry ingredients together. Add to batter and beat until smooth. Add lemon rind and nuts. Place in a greased, 4x8-inch pan and bake at 350 degrees for 1 hour. While bread is baking, mix lemon juice and sugar for glaze until sugar is dissolved. Spoon glaze over hot bread before removing from the pan. Continue until bread has absorbed all the glaze.

'SCONSET SPOON BREAD

2/3 cup stone-ground white cornmeal
2 cups light cream or milk
1 tbsp. butter
1 tsp. salt
2 tsp. sugar
1/2 tsp. baking powder
2 eggs, separated

Mix the first five ingredients together in a saucepan. Stir and cook over low heat until thickened to the consistency of thin oatmeal. Remove from the heat and cool to lukewarm. Preheat oven to 350 degrees. Grease a 1 1/2-quart casserole. Stir baking powder into cooled cornmeal mixture. Beat egg yolks slightly and add to mixture. Beat egg whties until stiff, and fold into batter. Pour into the prepared baking dish. Bake about 45 minutes, until top is lightly browned. Serve immediately, spooning from the baking dish, with butter. Consistency will be like custard. Yield: 6 servings

CRANBERRY BREAD

2 cups flour
1/2 tsp. salt
1/2 tsp. soda
1 1/2 tsp. baking powder
2 tbsp. butter
1 cup sugar
1 egg, beaten slightly
Juice of 1 orange
Grated rind of 1 orange
Boiling water
1 cup whole cranberries
1/2 cup chopped walnuts

Sift all dry ingredients together. Dust cranberries and nuts with flour. Place juice and rind of orange in a measuring cup and add boiling water to make 3/4 cup. Blend butter and sugar until creamy. Add slightly beaten egg, then orange juice mixture. Blend this with nuts and cranberries into dry ingredients. Place in a small, greased loaf pan and bake at 325 degrees for 1 hour. Yield: 1 loaf

BLUEBERRY BREAD

3 cups unsifted all purpose flour
2 tsp. baking powder
1 tsp. baking soda
1/2 tsp.salt
2/3 cup vegetable shortening
1 1/3 cups sugar
4 eggs
1/2 cup milk
1 1/2 tsp. lemon-juice
1 cup crushed pineapple, well drained
2 cups fresh blueberries, rinsed and drained
1 cup chopped walnuts or pecans
1/2 cup flaked coconut

Preheat oven to 350 degrees. Sift flour with baking powder, baking soda, and salt. Cream shortening until light and fluffy. Gradually beat in sugar. Stir in eggs, milk, lemon juice, and pineapple. Beat in dry ingredients. Fold in blueberries, nuts, and coconut. Pour dough into six greased and floured (6x3x2-inch) pans. Bake for 40–45 minutes.

CLASSIC BOSTON BROWN BREAD

1 cup rye flour
1 cup yellow cornmeal
1 cup whole wheat flour
1 tsp. salt
1 tsp. baking soda

3/4 cup unsulphured molasses
2 cups buttermilk
1 cup seedless raisins
Butter for pans and foil

Preheat oven to 350 degrees. Butter a 9x5-inch loaf pan and a length of foil to cover it. Sift the rye, cornmeal, whole wheat, and salt into a large bowl.

In a small bowl mix the baking soda with the molasses until it turns foamy. Mix in the buttermilk until well blended. Pour the molasses mixture into the flour mixture and mix well. Fold in the raisins. Pour the batter into the pan or cans and cover very tightly.

Bake for 1 hour or until a toothpick inserted in the center comes clean.

IRISH SODA BREAD

4 cups flour
1 tsp. baking soda
1 tsp. baking powder
1 tsp.salt
1 tsp. nutmeg
1 cup sugar

7 oz. muscat raisins*
1 stick butter, softened
1 cup buttermilk
2 eggs

Mix dry ingredients together in a large bowl. Add raisins and mix. Add butter, cutting into dry ingredients with a pastry blender. Add eggs to buttermilk and whisk together. Make a well in the center of the dry ingredients and pour buttermilk and egg mixture in dry ingredients. Mix well with a fork. Mixture will be moist. Form into a big ball and cut in half. Place each half into a greased and floured glass loaf baking dish.

Bake at 325 degrees for 1 hour. Toothpick will come out clean near middle. Do not over bake. After turning out on a rack, wrap right away in plastic wrap and let cool. It keeps it nice and moist. Freezes very well. Makes 2 loaves.

Note: Muscat raisins are available through Sun Maid in bulk. If using regular raisins, soak in hot water till they puff up. Drain before adding to dry ingredients.

Savor THE DAWN
BREAKFAST, BREADS, AND BRUNCH

CASSEROLE BREAD

4 cups white flour
1 tbsp. sugar
2 tsp. salt
1 tbsp. dry yeast
1 1/2 cups water

In a large mixing bowl stir into 2 cups of flour the yeast, sugar, and salt. Heat water to 105 degrees and beat into flour mixture with an electric mixer for 10 minutes. Add enough flour to make stiff dough. Divide between two greased, 1-quart casseroles. This can be baked in one large casserole as well. Cover with a kitchen towel and let rise until doubled. For a softer crust, brush with butter.

Bake in a preheated, 400-degree oven for about 40 minutes.

ROSEMARY RAISIN BREAD

1 cup whole wheat flour
2 cups white flour
1 tbsp. flax seed meal
1 tbsp. dry yeast
1 tsp. salt
1 tsp. dried whole rosemary
3 tbsp. sugar
1/2 cup milk
1/2 cup water
1/4 cup olive oil
2 eggs (one separated)
1/2 cup raisins

In a large mixing bowl stir together: wheat flour, flax, dry yeast, salt, rosemary, sugar, and half of the white flour. In a smaller bowl, microwave water, milk, and oil to 105 degrees. Add to dry ingredients and beat with an electric mixer, adding one whole egg and one egg white for 5 minutes. Reserve the yolk for glazing the loaf before baking.

Stir in the rest of the white flour and blend thoroughly. Turn onto a floured board and knead for ten minutes. (This can be done with an electric dough hook.) Add raisins.

Oil a large bowl with olive oil. Put dough into bowl and turn so that it becomes covered with the oil. Cover bowl with a clean dish towel and set aside to rise to double in bulk (about 1–1 1/2 hours).

Punch down. Knead slightly to get out excess air bubbles. Form into a rounded loaf and place on an olive oil-greased cookie sheet. Brush liberally with more oil. Cover and let rise about an hour.

Slash an "X" on the top with very sharp, floured knife. Brush with reserved yoke to which has been added 1 tablespoon of cold water. Bake in a preheated, 350-degree oven for 25–30 minutes. Makes 1 loaf.

THE INDIA HOUSE BANANA BREAD

3 ripe or overripe bananas (4 small)
1 cup sugar
1 egg
1 1/2 cups flour
1/4 cup melted butter
1 tsp. baking soda
1 tsp. salt

Preheat oven to 325 degrees.

Mash banana with a fork. Stir in remaining ingredients. Pour batter into Teflon-coated or buttered loaf pan. Bake 1 hour at 350 degrees.

ONION CHEESE PIE

2 (9-inch) unbaked pie shells (frozen or fresh)
1 cup sliced onions
2 tbsp. butter
3 eggs
1 1/2 cups milk
1 tsp. salt
Pepper
1/2 tsp. basil
2 cups grated Cheddar cheese

Sauté onions in butter. Beat eggs and add milk, salt, pepper, basil, and onions. Divide cheese in half and spread evenly in bottom of each pie crust. Pour milk mixture over cheese in both pies. Bake at 400 degrees for 40 to 45 minutes. Allow to set 5 minutes before serving.
Serves 6–8

CARDAMOM BRAID

5 cups white flour
1 1/2 tsp. ground cardamom seeds
1/2 cup sugar
1 tsp. salt
2 tsp. dry yeast
1/2 cup water
1/2 cup milk
1 1/2 cups butter or margarine
3 eggs (reserve one egg white for glaze)
1/2 cup raisins
2 tbsp. sugar for glaze

In a large mixing bowl, stir together 2 cups flour, cardamom, 1/2 cup sugar, salt, and yeast.

Heat the water, milk, and butter to 105 degrees. Add to flour mixture and beat with an electric mixer for 5 minutes, adding eggs and yolk during that time.

Stir in remaining flour. Turn onto a floured board and knead, adding raisins, for about 10 minutes. (A dough hook may be used in place of this step). Put into a large buttered bowl, turning dough to cover with butter. Cover the bowl with a kitchen towel and set aside to rise for about an hour, until doubled.

Punch down. Divide in half. Then divide each half into thirds. Shape each third into long strands and braid, pinching together the ends. Place each loaf on a greased cookie sheet. Cover with a towel and allow to rise until doubled, about 1 hour.

Before baking in a preheated, 350-degree oven, brush with a mixture of the 2 tbsp. sugar and egg white. Bake for about 35 minutes.

Savor THE DAWN
BREAKFAST, BREADS, AND BRUNCH

NONIE'S CORN BREAD

3/4 cup yellow cornmeal
1/3 cup sugar
3/4 tsp. salt
1 egg, beaten
1 cup flour
1 tbsp. baking powder
1 cup milk
2 tbsp. oil

Mix dry ingredients. Add liquids and egg. Mix until just moistened. Pour into a greased 8-inch square pan and bake in a 425-degree oven for 20 minutes.

Variations:
- substitute orange juice for milk and reduce sugar to 1/4 cup;
- substitute blue cornmeal for yellow and add 1/2 cup fresh, frozen, or dried blueberries;
- stir in 1 tablespoon jalapeño pepper, chopped;
- stir in 1/2 cup fresh, frozen, or dried cranberries, chopped.

QUICK CRAB QUICHE

1/2 cup mayonnaise
2 tbsp. all-purpose flour
2 eggs, beaten
1/2 cup milk
1 (7-oz.) can crabmeat, drained and flaked
8 oz. Swiss cheese, chopped (2 cups)
1/3 cup sliced scallions
1/4 tsp. thyme (optional)
1 (9-inch) pie crust, unbaked

Mix the mayonnaise, flour, eggs, and milk in a bowl. Stir in the crabmeat, cheese, scallions, and thyme. Pout into the pie shell. Bake at 350 degrees for 40 to 45 minutes or until set.

BRIE AND SAUSAGE SOUFFLÉ

6 slices white bread
1 lb. hot bulk pork sausage, browned and drained
3/4 lb. Brie cheese, rind removed and cubed
1 cup Parmesan cheese
5 eggs
2 cups whipping cream
2 cups milk
1 1/2 tbsp. chopped fresh sage
1 tsp. seasoned salt
1 tsp. dry mustard
2 eggs
1 cup whipping cream

Trim the crusts from the bread slices and place the crusts evenly on the bottom of a lightly greased 9x13-inch baking dish. Layer the bread slices, sausage, Brie, and Parmesan cheese in the baking dish. Whisk 5 eggs and 2 cups whipping cream in a bowl. Add the milk, sage, seasoned salt, and dry mustard and mix well. Pour over the bread layers. Chill, covered, for 8 hours. Whisk the 2 eggs and 1 cup whipping cream in a bowl. Pour over the prepared layers. Bake at 350 degrees for 1 hour or until the center is set and a knife inserted in the center comes out clean. You may substitute half-and-half for the whipping cream if desired. Yield: 8–10 servings.

APRICOT SQUARES

1/2 cup butter
1/4 cup sugar
1 cup sifted flour
1/2 tsp. baking powder
1/4 tsp. salt
1 cup light brown sugar
2 eggs, beaten
1/2 tsp. vanilla
1/2 cup chopped nuts
1/2 cup dried apricots
Confectioners' sugar

Snip apricots into small pieces and place in a saucepan with a little water. Steam for a short time until soft, but not sloppy. Mix first three ingredients until crumbly. Pack into a greased, 8-inch square pan and bake at 350 degrees for 25 minutes. Beat brown sugar and eggs. Add remaining dry ingredients and mix well. Blend in vanilla, nuts, and apricots. Spread over the baked layer. Bake again for 30 minutes. Cool. Cut into small bars, dipping the knife in ice water as you do so. Roll in confectioners' sugar.

GRANDMA VERA'S CHERRY COFFEE CAKE TORTE

1 cup butter or margarine
1 cup sugar
2 eggs
1 tsp. vanilla extract
1 tsp. almond extract
2 cups flour, sifted
2 tsp. baking powder
1/2 tsp. salt

1 can cherry-pie filling
3 tsp. butter, softened
1/4 cup sugar
1/4 cup flour
3/4 cup chopped nuts (optional)

Cream butter and sugar until fluffy. Add eggs and beat well. Add sifted dry ingredients and mix well. Batter will be very heavy. Spread half of the batter in a 9x13x2-inch pan and cover with the cherry-pie filling. Drop remaining batter over pie filling by spoonfuls and swirl gently over all. Combine last 4 ingredients by hand to make a streusel topping. Sprinkle the streusel mix over the entire cherry batter mix. Bake at 350 degrees for 45 minutes.

TOMATO PIE

2 large tomatoes, cut into 1/2-inch slices
1 (9-inch) baked pie crust
1/2 tsp. basil, chopped
1/2 tsp. fresh chives, chopped
1/2 cup mayonnaise
1 cup sharp Cheddar cheese, grated

Preheat oven to 350 degrees. Place tomato slices into pie crust, cutting pieces to fit so entire bottom is covered. Sprinkle with all the herbs.

Mix together mayonnaise and cheese and spread on top of tomatoes, sealing the edges with the mixture.

Bake for 35 minutes. When cool, cut into 6 or 10 wedges, depending on whether you are serving as an appetizer or as luncheon fare served with an accompaniment.
Serves 6–10

Savor
THE SEASONS
SOUPS AND CONDIMENTS

THE SOUP OF TOMATOES

1 (1-quart) can tomotoes
3/4 cup chopped celery
1/2 cup chopped carrots
1 small onion, chopped
1 green bell pepper, chopped
3 whole cloves
1 tsp. peppercorns
1 teaspoon salt
Dash of cayenne pepper
Dash of mace
3/4 cup whipping cream, whipped
Chopped fresh parsley

Combine the undrained tomatoes, celery, carrots, onion, bell pepper, cloves, peppercorns, salt, cayenne pepper, and mace in a saucepan. Simmer for 1 hour or until the vegetables are tender. Strain into a saucepan, but do not force the vegetables through the sieve as the soup should be clear. Cook until the soup is heated through. Ladle into bouillon cups. Dollop with the whipped cream. Sprinkle with chopped parsley. Serves 4–6

CAULIFLOWER SOUP

1 medium onion, chopped
1 cauliflower, cut into pieces, leaves and stems removed
1 carrot, peeled and diced
1 medium potato, peeled and diced
4–6 cups chicken broth
Nutmeg and cayenne pepper (optional)
2 tbsp. butter

Sauté onion in butter until translucent, about 7 minutes. Add cauliflower, carrot, potato, and broth. Bring to a boil over medium heat. Simmer 20 minutes or until vegetables are soft. Allow to cool. Purée in batches in a blender. Reheat on stove and add spices (optional).

CHICKEN AND WILD RICE SOUP

1/2 cup butter or margarine
2 stalks celery, thinly sliced
2 carrots, diced
1 medium onion, chopped
1/3 cup all-purpose flour
1 1/2 quart canned low-sodium chicken broth
1 tsp. sea salt (or kosher salt)
1/2 tsp. freshly ground pepper
2 cups chicken, cooked and chopped
2 cups cooked wild rice (or white rice)
1 cup heavy cream
1 tbsp. parsley, chopped

In a Dutch oven or stockpot, melt the butter. Add celery, carrots, and onion and cook, stirring constantly over medium heat. Heat for 5 minutes until vegetables are crispy-tender. Stir in flour and cook, stirring, until well mixed (about 5 minutes). Add chicken broth. Bring to a boil. Add salt and pepper, reduce heat and simmer for 10 minutes. Add chicken, rice, cream, and parsley. Cook until soup is thoroughly heated. Do not boil! This recipe can be doubled and frozen. Yield: 9 cups

ITALIAN SAUSAGE SOUP

1 1/2 lbs. medium-spiced Italian sausage, cut into 1/4-inch slices
2 garlic cloves, minced
2 onions, chopped
2 (16-oz.) cans stewed tomatoes
5 cups beef stock
1/2 tsp. basil
1/2 tsp. oregano
1 medium green bell pepper, seeded and chopped
2 medium zucchini, cut into 1/4-inch slices
2 cups uncooked bow tie pasta
Salt and pepper to taste
1/2 cup grated Parmesan cheese

Cook the sausage in a heavy 5-quart saucepan over medium heat for 7 to 10 minutes or until light brown. Remove the sausage with a slotted spoon. Drain the saucepan, reserving 3 tablespoons of the drippings. Add the garlic and onions. Sauté for 2 to 3 minutes. Return the sausage to the saucepan. Add the tomatoes, wine, stock, basil, and oregano. Simmer, uncovered, for 30 minutes. Add the bell pepper, zucchini, and pasta. Simmer, covered, for 25 minutes or until the pasta is al dente. Ladle into deep bowls and sprinkle with the Parmesan cheese. Serves 8–10

KALE SOUP

1/4 cup diced salt pork or diced bacon
1 tbsp. olive oil
2 large onions, diced
1 clove of fresh garlic, chopped
4 cups diced carrots (8–10 medium-sized carrots)
6 medium potatoes, peeled and cut into bite-sized pieces
1 pkg. linguiça or chouriço, cut in to bite-sized pieces
4 cups chicken stock, preferably homemade
1 cup beef stock
2 cups cold water
2 (10 oz.) pkgs. frozen kale, defrosted, or one head of fresh kale, chopped
1 can (19 ozs.) red kidney beans, drained and rinsed
1 can (19 ozs.) Cannellini or white kidney beans, drained and rinsed
1 tsp. salt
1 tsp. fresh ground pepper
1 tsp. paprika or red pepper flakes
1 meaty beef marrow or veal marrow bone

Dice the onions, carrots, potatoes, and meat into small bits. Using a heavy stockpot, drizzle a tablespoon of olive oil and add the diced bacon or salt pork and heat. As the bacon becomes cooked, add the diced onion, chopped garlic, and carrots. Sauté on low heat. If you have a meaty beef or veal marrow bone to add, that will enhance the flavor as well.

Place the diced potatoes in a separate pan, cover with cold water and bring to a boil. When the potatoes have boiled for 3 minutes, drain, rinse, and add to the sautéed vegetables in the stockpot. Add chicken stock, water, and beans to the stockpot and heat until it comes to a full boil. Reduce heat to a simmer. Add kale, salt, pepper, and paprika or red pepper flakes. Simmer for 30 to 40 minutes, adding more stock or fresh water as needed.

Variation: Traditional kale soup is made with turnips and cabbage instead of the potatoes and carrots. This soup freezes well.

CARROT DILL SOUP

2 tbsp. unsalted butter
1 medium onion, coarsely chopped
1 3/4 lb. carrots, cut into rings
3/4 lb. sweet potato
1/2 lb. baking potato
5 cups chicken stock

1 1/2 tsp. salt
1/2 tsp. pepper
1 tbsp. lemon juice
2 1/2 tbsp. chopped dill
Sour cream

Melt butter in a medium saucepan and brown the onions until a light golden color. Bake the sweet potato and baking potato at 400 degrees. Scoop from the skins and reserve the flesh. Scrape the sautéed onions into a food processor and add the chicken broth. Add carrots, sweet potato, baked potato, salt, pepper and lemon juice. Purée well. Pour the mixture into a saucepan with the stock and dill. Cook on low heat for 30 minutes. Serve warm with a dollop of sour cream.

SHERRIED MUSHROOM SOUP

1/2 lb. assorted mushrooms (portobello, porcini, or shiitake), sliced
1/3 cup finely chopped onion
3 tbsp. butter
2 tbsp. all-purpose flour
1 (10-oz.) can beef broth
2 cups half-and-half
1/4 cup dry sherry
1 tsp. dried basil, or 1 tbsp. chopped fresh basil
1/2 tsp. dried tarragon or 1 1/2 tsp. chopped fresh tarragon
Salt and pepper to taste

Sauté the mushrooms and onion in 2 tablespoons of the butter in a 2-quart saucepan over medium heat until tender. Remove the mushroom mixture to a bowl. Melt the remaining 1 tablespoon butter in the saucepan. Add the flour and cook for 1 minute, stirring constantly. Add the broth gradually, stirring constantly. Add the half-and-half gradually, stirring constantly. Cook until thickened, stirring frequently. Add the mushroom mixture, sherry, basil, tarragon, salt and pepper and mix well. Reduce the heat and simmer for 10 to 15 minutes or until heated through. Ladle into soup bowls. Serves 6

CURRIED BUTTERNUT SQUASH AND APPLE BISQUE

2 tbsp. unsalted butter
2 tbsp. extra-virgin olive oil
4 cups yellow onions (2 large), chopped
1 cinnamon stick
1 bay leaf
2 tbsp. mild curry powder
5 lb. butternut squash (2 large)
4 Granny Smith apples
2 tbsp. kosher salt
1/2 tsp. freshly ground black pepper
2 cups heavy cream
3 cups apple cider

Peel the squash, cut in half and remove the seeds. Cut the squash into large chunks. Toss with olive oil and roast on a cookie sheet in a 300-degree oven for 25 minutes or until tender. Do NOT brown.

Warm the butter, olive oil, onions, and curry powder in a large stockpot, uncovered, on low heat for 10–15 minutes, until the onions are tender. Stir occasionally, scraping the bottom of the pot. Peel, quarter, and core the apples. Cut into chunks.

Add the squash, apples, salt, pepper, bay leaf, cinnamon stick, and 3 cups of apple cider to the pot. Bring to a boil, cover, and cook over low heat for 20–30 minutes, until the squash and apples are soft. Remove from heat. Remove the cinnamon stick and bay leaf. Process the soup in a food processor fitted with a steel blade.

Pour the processed soup back into the pot on medium heat. Add the cream and enough water to make the soup the consistency you like. Bring to a light boil and reduce to simmer until ready to serve.

Taste the soup, it should be slightly sweet and thick. Add salt and pepper to taste. To sweeten your soup, add 2 teaspoons of brown sugar. Bring to a light boil and reduce to simmer until ready to serve.

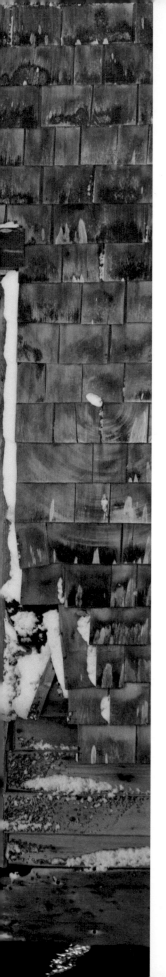

NEW ENGLAND (QUAHOG) CLAM CHOWDER

1 quart quahog clams, steamed in their liquor
1/4 lb. salt pork, cut into 1/2-inch pieces
3 medium onions, sliced very thin
4 medium potatoes, sliced very thin
4 cups milk
2 tbsp. butter
Salt and pepper to taste

Strain clam liquor through a strainer. Cut clams into approximately 1/2 -inch pieces.

In a large kettle, sauté the salt pork over medium heat until crisp. Remove pork, reserving fat in a pan. Drain and set aside. Add the onions to the fat and cook until tender and transparent. Add the potatoes and clam juice and enough water to just cover the potatoes. Simmer until potatoes are tender. Add the clams and the salt pork. Cook for 5 more minutes.

Heat the milk over medium heat in a separate saucepan with the butter. Do not boil. Add to the chowder. Add salt and pepper to taste.

Remove from the heat and serve. This chowder tastes even better the next day, but should be reheated with care so that it does not boil.   Serves 4–6

CORN CHOWDER

1 tbsp. olive oil
1/4 cup diced salt pork or diced bacon
1 large onion diced
1/2 cup diced red pepper
1/2 cup diced green pepper
4 cups chicken stock, preferably homemade
1 can cream-style corn
2 cans or 16 oz. frozen whole kernel corn
2 cups whole or evaporated milk
1 cup half-and-half or cream
1/2 tsp. salt
1 tsp. pepper, preferably white pepper
1 tsp. thyme (add a bit more if you have fresh thyme available)
1 tsp. nutmeg
1 tsp. paprika or red pepper flakes

Measure milk and set aside so it comes to room temperature while you are preparing the vegetables. Dice the bacon, onion, and peppers into small bits. Using a heavy stockpot, drizzle a tablespoon of olive oil and add the diced bacon or salt pork and heat. As the bacon becomes cooked, add the diced onion and peppers. Sauté on low heat.

Place the diced potatoes in a separate pan, cover with cold water and bring to a boil. When the potatoes have boiled for 3 minutes, drain, rinse, and add to the sautéed vegetables in the stock pot. Add chicken stock and corn. Heat through until it comes to a full boil. Turn down heat to a simmer. Fold in milk and half-and-half. Add salt, pepper, thyme, and paprika or red pepper flakes, and season to taste. If you have fresh thyme, use that instead of dried.

Simmer for 20 to 30 minutes adding more stock or cream as needed. Stir constantly so milk doesn't scald.

CHILLED SUMMER PEACH SOUP

6 large, ripe peaches
1 tbsp. honey
1 cup plain yogurt
1/3 cup peach nectar
1/8 cup Riesling wine
1 tbsp. crystallized ginger, minced
1 tbsp. fresh mint, chopped
1 tbsp. fresh chives, chopped
1/2 tsp. orange zest, minced
1 tsp. curry powder
Mint sprigs
Plain yogurt
24 raspberries

Place peaches in boiling water for 2 minutes. Remove from the heat and place in an ice-water bath. Gently pull off the skin. Halve and pit the peaches.

In a food processor or blender, purée the peaches, honey, yogurt, peach nectar, wine, crystallized ginger, mint, chives, orange zest, and curry powder.

Refrigerate, covered, for at least 2 hours. Adjust the sweetness level, adding a little more yogurt to make sure that the soup is not so sweet that it overpowers the wine. Ladle into soup bowls. Garnish with mint sprigs, a small dollop of yogurt, and 4 raspberries per bowl.

Serves 6 as an appetizer

PINEAPPLE MANGO SALSA

1 small pineapple, diced
1 ripe mango, diced
1 red pepper, diced
1/4 cup sliced scallions or chopped chives
2 tbsp. cilantro, chopped
2 fresh limes
2 tbsp. olive oil
1 tbsp. honey

Place the pineapple, mango, red pepper, scallions, and cilantro in a bowl. Add the juice from the 2 large, fresh limes. Add the olive oil and honey.

THREE-MELON SALSA

1/2 cup (1/2-inch pieces) cantaloupe
1/2 cup (1/2-inch pieces) honeydew melon
1/2 cup (1/2-inch pieces) watermelon
1/2 cup unseasoned rice vinegar
1/2 cup (1/2-inch pieces) red bell pepper
1 jalapeño chili pepper, de veined, seeded and minced
1/2 cup chopped fresh cilantro
1/4 cup vegetable oil
Salt and pepper to taste

Combine the cantaloupe, honeydew melon, watermelon, rice vinegar, bell pepper, jalapeño, cilantro, oil, salt, and pepper in a bowl and toss to mix well.
Yield: 3 cups

WARM RAISIN SAUCE

1/2 cup brown sugar
3 tbsp. cornstarch
1/4 tsp. salt
2 cups cider
1/2 cup golden raisins, halved
16 whole cloves
2 (2-inch) cinnamon sticks
2 tbsp. butter

Combine sugar, cornstarch, and salt in a saucepan. Stir in cider, raisins, cloves, and cinnamon (cloves and cinnamon could go in cheesecloth sack, optional).

Cook and stir for 10 minutes. Add 2 tbsp. of butter. Remove spices and serve hot. Can be made ahead. Great on ham or roast pork.

ZUCCHINI RELISH

10 cups finely chopped zucchini
4 cups onion, ground
5 tbsp. salt
2 1/2 cups vinegar
4 1/2 cups sugar
1 tbsp. each, nutmeg, dry mustard, turmeric, and cornstarch
1/2 tsp. pepper
2 tsp. celery salt
1 sweet green pepper, finely chopped
1 red pepper, finely chopped

Put zucchini, onion, and salt into a large bowl, and mix well. Let stand overnight. Drain and rinse in cold water. Drain again and put into a large kettle with the remaining ingredients. Bring to a boil and simmer, uncovered, stirring occasionally for 30 minutes, or until desired consistency is reached. Pour into 4 or 5 sterilized quart-sized jars and seal. Process 5 minutes in a hot-water bath.

MUSTARD PICKLES

10 large cucumbers
5 large onions
1/4 cup coarse salt
3 cups white sugar
3/4 cup flour
3 tsp. dry mustard
1/2 tsp. pepper
2 tsp. turmeric
1 tsp. celery seed
2 1/2 cups vinegar
2 cups water

Peel and seed the cucumbers. Chop them and put them into a large pot. Add pickling salt and let stand overnight. Drain in a colander and leave until sauce is made.

Mix flour, sugar, and spices. Add vinegar and water. Stir well and bring to boil in a large pot. Add well-drained vegetables to the sauce, bring to a boil, and let simmer for 10 minutes

Bottle, when hot, in sterilized jars, and seal. Once jars are open, store in the refrigerator.

CARAMEL GLAZED ORANGE SLICES

6 large navel oranges
2 tbsp. brandy
Grated zest of 1 small orange
1 cup sugar

Peel the navel oranges. Cut into 1/4-inch slices. Arrange in a single layer on a large platter. Sprinkle with the brandy and orange zest. Heat the sugar in a 10-inch skillet until melted and deep amber in color, stirring to dissolve any lumps. Drizzle over the oranges. Chill, covered, for 2 hours. Yield: 8–10 servings

RÉMOULADE SAUCE

3/4 cup mayonnaise
1 tsp. salt
2 tsp. dry mustard
6 scallions
2 celery stalks
3 sprigs parsley
1 tsp. paprika
2 drops Tabasco
1/2 tsp. tarragon
1 tbsp. catsup
1 garlic clove

Put all ingredients in a blender or food processor and mix. Refrigerate for 4 hours before serving. Use as a substitute for red shrimp cocktail sauce.

Savor

THE FRESHNESS

SALADS AND DRESSINGS

ALMOND BROCCOLI SALAD

4 cups finely chopped fresh broccoli
1 cup celery
1 cup red seedless grapes
1 cup green seedless grapes
8 slices bacon, crisp-cooked and crumbled
1/2 cup sliced scallions
1 cup mayonnaise
1/4 cup sugar
2 tbsp. cider vinegar
1/2 tsp. pepper
1/2 tsp. curry powder
2/3 cup slivered almonds, toasted

Combine the broccoli, celery, red grapes, green grapes, bacon, and scallions in a large salad bowl and toss to mix. Mix the mayonnaise, sugar, vinegar, pepper, and curry powder in a small bowl. Add to the broccoli mixture and toss to coat. Sprinkle with the almonds just before serving. Serves 8

MIACOMET PASTA SALAD

32 oz. rigatoni
1 red onion, thinly sliced
1 green bell pepper, chopped
1 red bell pepper, chopped
1/2 cup chopped fresh cilantro or parsley
2 lbs. cooked crabmeat, flaked
1 (8-oz.) bottle Italian salad dressing
1 1/2–2 cups mayonnaise or mayonnaise-style salad dressing
Salt and freshly ground pepper to taste

Cook the pasta according to the package directions; rinse and drain. Let stand until cool. Combine the onion, bell peppers, cilantro, and crabmeat in a large bowl and toss to mix. Add the salad dressing and mayonnaise and mix well. Add the pasta and toss to coat. Season with salt and pepper. Chill, covered, until ready to serve. Serves 12

CREAMY CUCUMBER SUMMER SALAD

3 English cucumbers, peeled and sliced
1 large Vidalia or white onion, thinly sliced and separated into rings
3 tbsp. salt
1 cup sour cream
2 tbsp. white vinegar
1 1/2 tbsp. sugar
2 garlic cloves, chopped
1/4 tsp. white pepper
Hungarian paprika to taste

Toss the cucumbers, onion, and salt in a bowl. Chill, covered, for 2 to 10 hours. Drain and press the excess moisture from the cucumbers and onion. Combine the cucumber mixture, sour cream, vinegar, sugar, garlic, and white pepper in a serving bowl and mix gently. Sprinkle with paprika and serve immediately. Serves 4

Savor THE FRESHNESS
SALADS AND DRESSINGS

CARROT AND RAISIN SALAD WITH CITRUS DRESSING

SALAD:
8 medium carrots, peeled and coarsely shredded
1/4 cup raisins
1/3 cup cashews, chopped

DRESSING:
3/4 cup reduced-fat sour cream
1/4 cup nonfat milk
1 tbsp. honey
1 tbsp. orange juice concentrate
1 tbsp. lime juice
Peel of one medium orange, grated
1/4 tsp. salt

In a small bowl, combine sour cream, milk, honey, orange juice concentrate, lime juice, orange peel, and salt. Blend well and set aside. In a large bowl, combine carrots and raisins. Pour over blended dressing and toss to coat. Cover and refrigerate for 30 minutes. Toss again before serving and top with the cashews. Serves 8

Savor THE FRESHNESS
SALADS AND DRESSINGS

GOLDEN BEET SALAD WITH PORT WINE VINAIGRETTE

SALAD:
2 to 3 medium golden beets
1/4 lb. mesclun greens
1/4 lb. bleu cheese (Great Hill), crumbled

In a large pot, boil the beets until tender. Drain and cool. Rub the beets with a towel to remove the skin. Slice them very thinly. Wash the greens and dry.

VINAIGRETTE:
1/2 bottle good-quality port
1/2 cup extra-virgin olive oil
1/4 cup champagne vinegar
1 tsp. shallots, finely chopped
1 clove garlic, finely chopped
Salt and pepper to taste

In a saucepan, reduce the port to a thick, syrupy consistency and cool. In a bowl, blend the olive oil, champagne vinegar, and port. Add remaining ingredients. Salt and pepper to taste.

Assembly: Lay a small mound of greens on a chilled plate and arrange the beet slices (divide slices equally among the plates). Dress with the vinaigrette and top with the bleu cheese.

FAMILY STYLE SALAD

by John O'Connor, Proprietor, The Atlantic Café

Lettuce mix, 1/2 romaine or 1/2 red leaf, or a
packaged mix of your choice
1/2 medium red onion, thinly sliced
1/4 cup olive oil
1/8 cup red wine vinegar
Romano cheese (finely grated)
1/2 to 1 tsp. garlic powder
Salt and pepper to taste

Toss the lettuce wtih half of the sliced red onions,
olive oil, and red wine vinegar. Add the grated
Romano cheese, garlic, salt and pepper and toss
again. Top salad with the remaining red onion
slices and serve. For a heartier salad, add sliced
salami and sliced provolone cheese.

CONTINENTAL SALAD

Weber Duck Sauce
1 cup oil
3/4 cup ketchup
1 tsp. onion juice
1/4 cup vinegar
1/2 tsp. pepper
1/3 cup sugar
1 tsp. lemon juice
1 lb. elbow macaroni, cooked
3 stalks celery, finely chopped
1 large green pepper, finely chopped
1 large onion, finely chopped
2 pimentos
2 (7-oz.) cans shrimp
2/3 cup mayonnaise
1/2 tsp. paprika
2 tbsp. sugar
2 tbsp. vinegar

Mix the first eight ingredients together and add to the cooked elbow macaroni. Let marinate overnight. Add celery, green pepper, onion, pimentos, and shrimp. In a small bowl, blend together mayonnaise, paprika, sugar, and vinegar. Add to the salad.

Note: Crabmeat can be substituted for the shrimp. Or you can use 1 can crab with 1 can shrimp.

NEW POTATO AND GREEN BEAN SALAD

1/4 cup balsamic vinegar
2 tbsp. Dijon mustard
2 tbsp. fresh lemon juice
1 garlic clove, minced
Dash of Worcestershire sauce
1/2 cup extra-virgin olive oil
Salt and pepper to taste
1 1/2 lbs. small red potatoes
12 oz. green beans, trimmed
1 small red onion, coarsley chopped
1/4 cup chopped fresh basil

Whisk the vinegar, Dijon mustard, lemon juice, garlic, and Worcestershire sauce in a medium bowl. Add the olive oil gradually, whisking constantly. Season with salt and pepper. The dressing may be prepared 1 day ahead. Cover and refrigerate. Bring to room temperature and whisk before using.

Steam the potatoes until tender. Cool and cut into quarters. Cook the green beans in boiling salted water in a large saucepan for 5 minutes or until tender; drain. Plunge immediately into a bowl of ice water to cool; drain. Cut the green beans into halves. Combine the green beans, potatoes, onion, and basil in a large bowl. Add the dressing and toss to coat. Season with salt and pepper. Serve immediately, or cover and let stand at room temperature for up to 4 hours before serving.
Yield: 6 servings

WATERCESS AND HEARTS OF PALM SALAD

1 (14-oz.) can hearts of palm
3 bunches watercress, rinsed, trimmed
1 1/2 lbs. fresh mushrooms, sliced
5 oz. sliced almonds, toasted
2/3 cup vegetable oil
1/3 cup cider vinegar
2 tsp. sugar
1 tsp. salt
1 tbsp. drained capers
2 tbsp. grated onion
1 1/2 tsp. parsley flakes
1 hard-cooked egg, finely chopped
Dash of red pepper

Drain the hearts of palm. Cut into 1/4-inch slices. Combine the
watercress, mushrooms, hearts of palm, and almonds in a large salad
bowl and toss to mix. Serves 10

SHRIMP AND VEGETABLE PASTA SALAD

1 1/2 lbs. large shrimp, cooked and peeled
8 oz. tri-color rotelle, cooked and drained
8 oz. fresh green beans, cooked
4 tomatoes, peeled and chopped
1 (2-oz.) can sliced black olives, drained
2 tbsp. scallions, thinly sliced
1/2 cup fresh basil, slivered
2 tsp. garlic, minced
Salt and freshly ground pepper to taste
3 tbsp. balsamic vinegar
1/4 cup extra-virgin olive oil
5 to 6 cups mixed salad greens

Combine the shrimp, pasta, green beans, tomatoes, black olives,
scallions, basil, and garlic in a large bowl and mix gently. Sprinkle with
salt and pepper. Blend the vinegar and olive oil in a bowl. Pour over
the shrimp mixture and toss to coat. Adjust the seasonings. Serve
over the salad greens. Serves 4–6

STRAWBERRY SPINACH SALAD

1/2 cup sugar
1/2 cup vegetable oil
1/4 cup cider vinegar
1/4 tsp. Worcestershire sauce
2 tbsp. sesame seeds, toasted
1 tbsp. poppy seeds
1 1/2 tbsp. red onion, minced
2 bunches spinach, trimmed
2 cups sliced strawberries
1/2 cup roasted sunflower seeds

Dissolve the sugar in the oil, cider vinegar, and Worcestershire sauce in a bowl. Add the sesame seeds, poppy seeds, and red onion and mix well.

Rinse the spinach and pat dry. Tear into bite-sized pieces. Combine the spinach, strawberries, and sunflower seeds in a salad bowl. Add the dressing just before serving and toss to coat. Serves 8

CAESAR SALAD

1/2 cup olive oil
1/4 cup lemon juice
1 tbsp. Dijon mustard
1 1/2 tsp. Worcestershire sauce
1/2 cup shredded Parmesan cheese
Salt and pepper to taste
1 clove garlic, chopped
1 head of romaine lettuce
1 pkg. Caesar salad croutons
5 hard-boiled eggs

Mix first seven ingredients together. Wash and tear up lettuce into a bowl. Slice hard-boiled eggs. Combine all ingredients to complete the salad.

ORZO SALAD

16 oz. orzo pasta
1/4 cup olive oil
1 (10-oz.) pkg. frozen baby peas, thawed
1 red bell pepper, chopped
1 green bell pepper, chopped
3/4 cup chopped green onions
1 (4-oz.) can chopped black olives
1/4 cup chopped green olives
2/3 cup balsamic vinegar
3 tbsp. Teriyaki sauce
1 tbsp. soy sauce
10 oz. feta cheese, crumbled

Cook the pasta according to the package directions and drain. Add the olive oil to the pasta and toss to coat. Stir in the peas, bell peppers, green onions, and olives.

Whisk the vinegar, teriyaki sauce, and soy sauce in a bowl until blended. Add the vinegar mixture to the pasta mixture and toss to coat. Chill until serving time. Adjust the seasonings. Sprinkle with the cheese just before serving.

PICNIC COLESLAW

10 cups shredded green cabbage (about1 head)
1 large green bell pepper, thinly sliced
2 medium Spanish onions, thinly sliced
1 cup sugar
1 tsp. dry mustard
2 tsp. sugar
1 tsp. celery seeds
1 tbsp. salt
1 cup white vinegar
3/4 cup vegetable oil

Layer the cabbage, bell pepper, and onions in a large salad bowl. Sprinkle with 1 cup sugar. Combine the dry mustard, 2 teaspoons sugar, celery seeds, salt, vinegar, and oil in a saucepan and mix well. Bring to a boil, stirring constantly. Pour over the vegetable layers. Chill, covered, for 4 to 12 hours. Toss the coleslaw to mix just before serving.

Serves 12

Savor THE FRESHNESS
SALADS AND DRESSINGS

MUSSEL SALAD WITH RED BELL PEPPER

1 red pepper, roasted, peeled and diced
1 large tomato, peeled, seeded and diced
1 small red onion, diced
2 tbsp. capers
1/4 cup olive oil
1 tbsp. balsamic vinegar
4 lbs. mussels
1 cup white wine
2 cloves garlic, minced

Combine first six ingredients for the dressing; set aside for at least 30 minutes. Clean mussels thoroughly, discarding any that are not tightly shut. Cook in the white wine and garlic for 5 minutes. Remove from heat and drain. Discard any mussels that are not open. Remove the empty half shell and place each mussel in its half shell on a large platter. Spoon a small amount of dressing into each mussel. Serve with crusty bread. Serves 4–5

RICE TACO SALAD

1 lb. ground beef
1/2 onion, finely chopped
1 clove garlic, minced
1/2 tsp. salt
1/4 tsp. pepper
1/2 tsp. cumin

2 cups cooked white rice
1/2 head of lettuce, shredded
2 tomatoes, coarsely chopped
1/2 cup (2 oz.) Cheddar cheese, shredded
1 large avocado, chopped
1/4 cup sour cream

Brown the ground beef in a large skillet over medium heat, stirring until crumbly. Add the onion and garlic. Cook until the onion is tender, but not brown; drain. Add the salt and pepper, cumin, and rice and mix well. Remove from the heat to cool.

Combine the lettuce, tomatoes, cheese, avocado, and ground-beef mixture in a large bowl. Add the sour cream and toss lightly to coat. Serve immediately with picante sauce and corn chips. Serves 6

Savor THE FRESHNESS
SALADS AND DRESSINGS

WARM POTATO SALAD WITH OLIVES AND LEMON

by Chef Thomas Proch, the Club Car

1 1/2 lb. Yukon Gold or Ruby Crescent potatoes
Coarse salt
2 tbsp. dry vermouth
1/2 cup Kalamata olives, pitted
4 scallions, including greens, chopped
Zest of 1 lemon, grated
Fresh cracked pepper
2 tbsp. olive oil
Coarse sea salt

Scrub the potatoes. Place whole and unpeeled in a saucepan. Cover with cold water by at least an inch. Place over high heat and add a good pinch of salt. Bring to a boil. Remove cover part of the way, reduce heat to medium and cook until tender(about 20 minutes). Drain on a rack and let potatoes cool enough to handle. They must stay warm, so work quickly.

Peel the poatoes and cut into thick slices (about 1/2 inch). As you finish each one, place it in a mixing bowl and sprinkle with dry vermouth. Add the olives, scallions, and grated lemon zest. Season with pepper and drizzle with olive oil.

Transfer to a serving platter and sprinkle with sea salt. Serves 4

ROASTED POTATO AND CARROT SALAD
WITH BASIL-CITRUS DRESSING

3 lbs. small new or purple potatoes, rinsed
1 1/2 lbs. carrots, peeled
2 tbsp. olive oil
3/4 tsp. kosher salt
1/2 tsp. freshly ground pepper
1 lb. cherry tomatoes, halved (mixed red and yellow if available)

DRESSING:
3 scallions, minced
3/4 cup fresh basil, chopped
1 tbsp. fresh lemon juice
3 tbsp. fresh orange juice
1/2 tbsp. fresh lime juice
3/4 cup sour cream
1 tbsp. Dijon mustard
1/2 tbsp. honey
1/4 tsp. jalapeño-flavored Tabasco or other hot sauce
1/4 cup olive oil
Kosher salt and freshly ground pepper

Preheat oven to 375 degrees. Prick the potatoes in several places with a fork. Place potatoes and carrots in a large oven-proof dish or baking sheet. Drizzle with oil, using hands to coat the vegetables. Sprinkle with salt and pepper. Roast for 1 hour. Remove from the oven and cool. Quarter the potatoes and cut the carrots into 1-inch, bite-sized pieces. Place in a large, nonreactive bowl. Add the tomatoes.

To prepare the dressing, combine the green onions, basil, citrus juices, sour cream, mustard, honey, and Tabasco and whisk thoroughly. Add olive oil in a slow drizzle while whisking. Season to taste. Add the dressing to the potato mixture and mix thoroughly to coat the vegetables. Season to taste. Refrigerate for 2 to 3 hours, covered, before serving. Serve at room temperature. Serves 6

Savor THE FRESHNESS
SALADS AND DRESSINGS

WARM SCALLOP SALAD AND CHAMPAGNE BEURRE BLANC

by Chef Eric Widmer, La Cumbre Country Club, Palm Springs, CA

2 tbsp. minced shallots
3/4 cup Champagne
1 cup (2 sticks) butter, cut into small pieces
12 (10- to 20-count) scallops
Salt to taste
2 tbsp. olive oil
4 oz. button mushrooms, cut into quarters
White portion of 1/2 a leek, sliced
1 tomato, peeled, seeded, and chopped
1 clove of garlic, minced
2 tbsp. rice vinegar
White pepper to taste
6 tbsp. olive oil
6 cups mixed salad greens

Combine the shallots and Champagne in a saucepan. Cook until reduced to *sec* (French for dry). Whisk in the butter, 1 piece at a time.

Season the scallops with salt. Sauté in 2 tablespoons olive oil in a skillet until brown. Remove the scallops from the skillet. Add the mushrooms to the skillet. Sauté until golden brown. Add the leek and tomato. Drain any excess liquid. Add the butter sauce and scallops. Simmer for 2 to 3 minutes or until the scallops are tender.

Combine the garlic, vinegar, salt, and white pepper in a bowl. Whisk in 6 tablespoons olive oil. Pour over the mixed salad greens in a salad bowl and toss to mix gently.

Arrange the scallops on individual salad plates. Pour the sauce over the scallops. Distribute the salad greens evenly on the plates. Serve immediately. Serves 4

SUMMERTIME SALAD

1/4 cup finely chopped green bell pepper
1/4 cup finely chopped cucumber
2 tsp. minced onion
1 cup sour cream
1/2 cup mayonnaise
1 tbsp. tarragon vinegar
1 tbsp. sugar
1 tsp. salt
1/2 tsp. black pepper
1 clove garlic, minced
1 tbsp. butter
1/2 cup sesame seeds
1/3 cup grated Parmesan cheese
Assorted varieties of lettuce

Combine the bell pepper, cucumber, onion, sour cream, mayonnaise, vinegar, sugar, salt, pepper, and garlic in a bowl and mix well. Chill, covered, in the refrigerator.

Melt the butter in a baking pan. Spread the sesame seeds and cheese in the butter. Bake at 350 degrees until brown, stirring frequently. Remove from the oven to cool.

Tear the lettuce into bite-sized pieces and place in a salad bowl. Pour the dressing over the lettuce mixture and toss to coat. Sprinkle with the sesame seed mixture and toss to mix. Serves 8

RASPBERRY VINAIGRETTE

1 1/2 tbsp. Dijon mustard
8 oz. raspberry vinegar
1 1/2 cup light olive oil
2 tbsp. shallots, chopped
1 tbsp. chives, chopped
1 tbsp. chopped parsley
2 tsp. chopped thyme
1 1/2 tbsp. honey
Salt and pepper to taste

Start with the Dijon mustard. Alternatively whisk in oil and vinegar to emulsify. Add the rest of the ingredients and mix well. This recipe is best done with fresh herbs the day before to let flavors blend, but still good freshly made. Also, try using other vinegar flavors such as champagne, sherry, or balsamic.

ORANGE-BALSAMIC SALAD DRESSING

1/4 cup olive oil
2 tbsp. balsamic vinegar
1 tbsp. light brown sugar
Peel of one orange, finely shredded
1 tbsp. honey
1/2 tsp. salt

Whisk together all ingredients until brown sugar dissolves.

Savor
THE FARM

VEGETABLES AND SIDE DISHES

BUTTER BALLS FOR VEGETABLES

1 lb.(4 sticks) butter
4 envelopes of chicken broth
2 tbsp. parsley flakes
1/4 tsp. savory leaves
1/4 tsp. basil
1/4 tsp. marjoram
1/4 tsp. tarragon
2 tsp. seasoned salt
2 tsp. regular salt
1/2 cup lemon juice

Melt butter. Add all other ingredients, mixing well. Freeze in a square pan. When frozen, cut into pats. Store frozen. Add to any vegetables when cooking.

SURFSIDE SWEET POTATOES

6 large sweet potatoes
1 cup butter
1/2 cup bourbon
1 cup walnuts
1 tsp. salt

Bake the sweet potatoes on a cookie sheet in a 400-degree oven until soft. Scoop out the pulp. Beat with a mixer until soft.

In a saucepan, heat 3/4 cup butter, the bourbon, and the salt over low heat. Add the potatoes and beat until blended.

Turn into a greased baking dish. Dot with remaining butter, sprinkle with the walnuts. Bake in a preheated 350-degree oven for 20 minutes.
Yield: 8 servings

BARTLETT FARM GRILLED GREEN BEANS WITH WARM GORGONZOLA VINAIGRETTE

by Chef All Kovalencik, Company of the Cauldron

1 lb. green beans (5 cups)
1 tsp. olive oil
1/4 cup balsamic vinaigrette
1/4 cup crumbled Gorgonzola cheese
1 tsp. brown sugar
3/4 tsp. chopped garlic
3/4 tsp. chopped shallots
1/2 tsp. fresh thyme, chopped (1/4 tsp. dried)
1/2 tsp. fresh basil (1/4 tsp. dried)
Salt and pepper

Preheat grill, gas or charcoal.

To prepare green beans, I prefer to snap just the stem end, leaving the beautiful line and point of the bean intact. I always blanch beans before grilling or sautéeing them. Blanching beans keeps them bright green, and ensures that they won't be overcooked. Leaving a bean too raw keeps it from exuding its natural sweetness, just as surely as overcooking destroys its texture.

In a medium saucepan, bring about 6 cups of lightly salted water to a boil. Add the beans and blanch them for 4 minutes. Drain the beans in a colander and immediately immerse them in an ice-water bath to stop the cooking process.

In a small saucepan, combine 1 tsp. olive oil and all the remaining ingredients. Warm over medium heat until the ingredients start to combine, about 7 minutes. Toss the green beans in the remaining olive oil and season lightly with salt and pepper.

Quickly grill the beans on a hot charcoal or gas grill, about 30 seconds on each side. Toss the beans in the warmed vinaigrette and serve immediately. Serves 4–6

SPINACH PROVENÇAL

by the Caron brothers, Father Paul and Chef David Caron

4 tbsp. olive oil
1 medium Spanish onion, diced small
6 cloves garlic, peeled and sliced
2 tomatoes, seeded and diced large
4 oz. fresh spinach, washed and stems removed
Salt and freshly cracked pepper to taste

Heat olive oil in a heavy pan over medium heat. When oil is hot, add onion and sauté until translucent, 3 to 4 minutes. Add sliced garlic and sauté until edges brown lightly. Add chopped tomatoes, stir and sauté for 1 minute more. Add spinach, cover and reduce heat to low. Sweat for 2 minutes. Stir, folding over ingredients. Sauté 1 more minute and turn off heat. Add salt and freshly cracked pepper to taste.

Savor THE FARM
VEGETABLES AND SIDE DISHES

PAN-GLAZED PARSNIPS WITH SHERRY

1 lb. parsnips, peeled
1/2 cup chicken stock or water
2 tbsp. unsalted butter
2 tbsp. dry sherry or Madeira
2 tsp. fresh ginger, peeled and minced
1 tsp. chopped fresh thyme, or 1/4 tsp. dried thyme
Salt to taste
Few drops of lemon juice
Freshly ground pepper to taste

Cut the parsnips in half lengthwise, then cut the halves in half again if they are very thick. Cut the pieces in half crosswise so you have finger-length sticks that are more or less the same thickness. If the cores are distinctly darker and denser than the rest of the root, remove them with a paring knife.

Put the parsnips in a frying pan large enough to hold them in a single layer. Add the stock or water, butter, sherry or Madeira, ginger, and thyme. Season with salt. Partially cover the pan and place over medium heat. Bring to a simmer and cook until the parsnips are tender enough to be easily pierced with the tip of a paring knife, 7 to 9 minutes.

Uncover the pan, raise the heat to high, and continue to cook, uncovered, until the juices are reduced to a glaze, 4 to 6 minutes. Season with the lemon juice and a few grinds of pepper. Taste and adjust the seasonings. Transfer the parsnips to a warmed serving dish and serve immediately. Serves 3–4

Savor THE FARM
VEGETABLES AND SIDE DISHES

STRING BEANS MARINATED WITH CORN AND CARROTS

3 lbs. fresh green beans
2/3 cup fresh carrots, grated
1/2 cup scallions, finely chopped
1 cup green peppers, finely chopped
2/3 cup celery, sliced
1 can whole kernel corn
1 small jar pimento strips
1 clove garlic, mashed
1/2 cup vinegar
1/4 cup water
1/2 cup sugar
1/2 cup salad oil
Salt and pepper, to taste

French cut the green beans and cook until barely tender. Drain and set aside. Combine all the vegetables in a bowl. Mix vinegar, water, sugar, garlic, salt, pepper, and salad oil. Pour over vegetables and add to beans. Marinate, stirring once a day for two or three days. Serve chilled.

SWEET PICKLED BEETS

3 lbs. beets, small fresh or small whole canned
1 onion, thinly sliced
3 cups sugar
3 cups vinegar
2 whole cloves for each jar (8 total)
2 bay leaves for each jar (8 total)

Simmer the beets until still crisp. Peel and slice. Bring the sugar and vinegar to a boil. Turn off the heat. Sterilize the jars (4 pints/8 cups). Fill the jars with the beets and sliced onion. Cover the beets with the syrup mixture. Add the cloves and bay leaf to each jar. Cover to seal the jars.

GLAZED PEARL ONIONS WITH RAISINS AND ALMONDS

2 lbs. pearl onions
1 cup dry sherry
1/2 cup raisins
1/4 cup honey
1/4 cup water
2 tbsp. butter
1 tsp. fresh thyme or 1/2 tsp. dry thyme
2/3 cup slivered almonds, toasted
4 tsp. sherry wine vinegar or red wine vinegar

Bring pot of salted water to boil. Add onions. Cook 3 minutes to loosen skins.
Drain and cool. Cut root ends from onions. Squeeze onions at stem end to
slip them out of their skins.

Combine onions, sherry, raisins, honey, water, butter, and thyme in a large
heavy skillet. Bring to a boil over medium-high heat. Reduce heat to very
low. Cover and simmer until onions begin to caramelize, stirring often, about
45 minutes. Season with salt and pepper and remove from heat. Onions
can be prepared to this point. Cover and refrigerate. Reheat over low heat
before continuing.   Stir in almonds and vinegar. Add a few drops of water if
too dry. Serve warm.

Note: Leftovers can be transformed into a great chutney. Simply cook with
diced Granny Smith apples.

ROASTED ONIONS

4 medium yellow onions, unpeeled and cut in half
2 tbsp. olive oil
Salt and freshly ground pepper

Set oven rack to lowest position. Heat oven to 425 degrees. Toss
onions with oil and salt and pepper. Place onions, cut-side down, on
a baking sheet. Roast until onions are tender and the cut sides are a
golden brown, 30 to 35 minutes.

Add salt and pepper if needed. Do not remove the skins.

Savor THE FARM
VEGETABLES AND SIDE DISHES

BRAISED LEEKS

4 medium leeks
1 2/3 cup tomato-vegetable juice
3 long strips of orange zest
2/3 cup orange juice
1/2 tsp. dried thyme
1/4 tsp. cinnamon
1/4 tsp. ground allspice
1/4 tsp. cayenne pepper
1 tbsp. extra-virgin olive oil
1/2 tsp. salt
2 tbsp. diced yellow or red bell pepper

Trim the root ends off each leek, being careful to
keep the leeks intact. Trim the tough, dark green tops
off, then quarter each leek lengthwise up to, but not
through, the root. Swish the leeks in a bowl of lukewarm
water easing the leaves apart to remove the grit.
Lift out the leeks, leaving the grit behind; repeat as
needed with clean water. Set aside.

In a large skillet, combine the tomato-vegetable juice,
orange zest, orange juice, thyme, cinnamon, allspice,
and cayenne. Bring to a boil over medium heat;
reduce to a simmer, and add the leeks. Cover and
cook until the leeks are tender, about 30 minutes.

With a slotted spoon, transfer the leeks to a serving
platter. Add the oil and salt to the sauce in the skillet.
Return to a boil over high heat, and cook, stirring
constantly, for 1 minute. Spoon the sauce over the
leeks, sprinkle the bell pepper on top and serve. Can
be served warm, room temperature, or chilled.

BAKED CARROTS

1 (1-lb.) bag fresh carrots
1/2 tsp. nutmeg
1-2 tbsp. sugar
Dabs of butter

Preheat oven to 325 degrees. Butter bottom and sides of a glass baking dish (7 1/2 x 11- inch/2 quart). Wash, peel, and cut carrots into 1-inch chunks. For large carrots, cut the piece on the diagonal to give better size. Add carrots to the baking dish along with enough water to just cover the bottom of the baking dish. Sprinkle the nutmeg and sugar over the top of the carrots. Take several small pieces, or dabs, of butter and place on top of the carrots. Cover the baking dish with aluminum foil and place in 325-degree oven. Bake for 1-1/2 hours, turning carrots and tossing with the sauce from the baking dish approximately halfway through the cooking process. Recover and return to the oven and continue cooking until carrots are cooked through. Serves 6

LIMA BEANS, ITALIAN STYLE

3 cups fresh, cooked lima beans or 1(16 oz.) pkg. frozen
1 clove garlic
4 tbsp. olive oil
2/3 cup canned tomatoes
1 cup hot water
1 celery stalk, chopped
Freshly ground pepper
Pinches: dried oregano, dried red pepper flakes, and dried mint
Salt and pepper to taste
Freshly grated Parmesan cheese

Drain beans well or, if using frozen beans, defrost. In a medium saucepan, sauté the garlic in the olive oil. Add the tomatoes and seasonings. Simmer for 5 minutes, stirring often. Add the water, and let the sauce come to a boil. Add the beans and the celery. Stir well, and let boil gently for a minute or two. Taste and add more seasonings, if desired. Cover and gently boil for about 30 minutes, or until the beans are tender. Do not overcook. Sprinkle with grated cheese and serve.

Savor THE FARM
VEGETABLES AND SIDE DISHES

CAULIFLOWER MILANESE

5 cups cauliflower florets
1/2 cup chicken or vegetable broth
3/4 tsp. grated lemon zest
1/2 tsp. salt
1/2 tsp. dried marjoram
1/4 tsp. freshly ground black pepper
1/4 cup plain dried bread crumbs
2 tbsp. grated Parmesan cheese
1 tsp. olive oil or butter
2 tsp. fresh lemon juice

Preheat oven to 400 degrees. In a large pot of boiling water, cook the cauliflower for 4 minutes to blanch. Drain well.

Meanwhile, in a small bowl, combine the broth, lemon zest, salt, marjoram, and pepper. Set aside. In another small bowl, combine the bread crumbs and Parmesan. Set aside.

Spread the oil or butter in a 13x9-inch baking dish and heat in the oven until hot, about 4 minutes. Add the cauliflower to the baking dish and bake, stirring occasionally, for 7 minutes, or until the cauliflower is golden. Pour the reserved broth mixture over the cauliflower and bake for 7 minutes, or until the cauliflower is tender. Sprinkle the bread crumb mixture over the cauliflower. Drizzle with the lemon juice and bake for 5 minutes, or until the topping is lightly crisped. Serves 4

ROASTED FALL VEGETABLES

3 cups turnips (about 1 1/4 lbs), peeled and cubed
3 cups sweet potato (about 1 1/4 lbs), peeled and cubed
2 1/2 cups Granny Smith apples (about 1 1/2 lbs), peeled and cubed
1 cup dried cranberries
1/2 cup dark brown sugar
1 tbsp. freshly squeezed lemon juice
2 tbsp. butter or margarine, cut into small pieces
Cooking spray

Preheat oven to 350 degrees. Combine the turnips, sweet potato, apple, cranberries, brown sugar, and lemon juice in a 2-quart baking dish coated with cooking spray. Top with butter and cook for 1 1/2 hours or until tender. Stir after 45 minutes.

HARVEST TORTA

10 slices white bread, toasted
8 oz. shredded Swiss cheese (2 cups)
8 oz. shredded fontinella cheese (2 cups)
8 oz. shredded Cheddar cheese (2 cups)
4 carrots, sliced
2 onions, chopped
2 tomatoes, chopped
2 yellow zucchini, sliced
2 green zucchini, sliced
1 small eggplant, sliced and sautéed (optional)
2 tbsp. olive oil

Crumble the toasted bread. Mix the Swiss cheese, fontinella cheese, and Cheddar cheese in a bowl. Layer 1/3 of the bread crumbs, carrots, 1/2 of the onions, tomatoes, 1/2 of the cheese mixture, 1/2 of the remaining bread crumbs, the remaining onions, yellow zucchini, green zucchini, remaining cheese mixture, eggplant, and remaining bread crumbs in a 9x13-inch baking dish. Drizzle with the olive oil. Bake at 350 degrees for 45 minutes. Serves 10–12

Savor THE FARM
VEGETABLES AND SIDE DISHES

BAKED CELERY CASSEROLE

5 celery stalks
1 onion, chopped
1 can sliced water chestnuts, drained
1 small jar chopped pimentos
1 can cream of mushroom soup
3/4 to1 cup slivered almonds
2 to 3 cups bread crumbs
1/2 cup butter

Blanch celery in boiling water for 7 minutes. Remove and drain. Sauté onion in 4 tablespoons of the butter. Mix celery, onion, pimentos, and cream of mushroom soup. Place mixture in a glass casserole dish.

Sauté almonds and bread crumbs together in the remaining butter. Spread on top of the celery mixture. Bake at 350 degrees for 15 minutes. Serves 8

LEMON-SCENTED PASTA PUDDING

8 oz. orzo, or another small, rice-shaped pasta
4 to 6 tbsp. butter, melted
Grated zest of 2 organic lemons
Juice of 1 lemon
2 cups ricotta cheese
3 to 4 tbsp. Greek yogurt or sour cream
1 to 1 1/4 cups sugar
3 eggs, lightly beaten
1/4 tsp. baking soda

Preheat oven to 375 degrees. Cook the pasta in a large pot of rapidly boiling, salted water until al dente, and drain. Toss with the butter and set aside. In a medium bowl, combine the lemon zest with the lemon juice, ricotta cheese, yogurt, sugar, eggs, and baking soda. Spoon into a large, shallow baking dish.

Bake for about 30 minutes, or until the top is lightly browned and caramelized in spots and the pudding is no longer wobbly, but is not completely firm; you want it to keep a soft, yielding texture. Serve hot or at room temperature. Serves 4–6

MOLDED RICE WITH SPINACH AND PARMESAN CHEESE

2 cups water
1 cup rice
4 oz. fresh spinach or Swiss chard
4 tbsp. fresh parsley, minced
1/2 tsp. salt
Freshly ground pepper
Freshly grated nutmeg
2 tbsp. heavy cream
1 1/2 oz. Parmesan cheese, freshly grated
1 carrot, cooked, notched lengthwise,
      and sliced crosswise in flower shapes

Bring water to a boil, add rice, and simmer covered for about 16–18 minutes. Wash the spinach and remove the center rib. Wilt spinach in a skillet, using only the water clinging to the leaves from washing. Cool and squeeze by the handful to remove any remaining water. Finely chop the spinach and parsley together. Blend with the salt, pepper, nutmeg, and heavy cream. Add along with the Parmesan cheese to the rice.

To serve, pack into individual molds with a carrot slice in the bottom. Leave in molds for 3 minutes, invert onto a plate, and tap the side of the mold to help it release.
Serves 6

SCALLOPED TURNIP

4 tbsp. butter
1/2 cup onion, thinly sliced
4 cups white turnip, thinly sliced
2 Tbsp. flour
1 tsp. salt
1 tsp. pepper
1 cup milk
1/2 cup cream

Butter a 1-quart casserole. Melt 1 tbsp. butter and lightly sauté onions until just wilted. Layer a third of the sliced turnip in the casserole, top with a third of the onion, sprinkle with 2 tsp. flour and 1/3 tsp. salt and pepper. Pat with 1 tbsp. butter, repeat making three layers. Mix milk and cream, pour over turnip. Cover and bake at 350 degrees for 30 minutes. Uncover and cook 30–45 minutes until tender and bubbly.

To make au gratin, top with 3/4 cup shredded Cheddar when you remove the cover.

This recipe can be made ahead until almost cooked, then put back in the oven to reheat, 20–30 minutes. Should look like scalloped potatoes when done.

EGGPLANT PARMIGIANA

by John O'Connor, Proprietor, The Atlantic Café

3 to 4 medium eggplants
2 (28-oz.) cans crushed tomatoes
2 tbsp. olive oil
Spray olive oil
1 lb. Parmesan cheese, finely grated
1 lb. shredded mozzarella cheese
1 (15-oz.) pkg. Italian bread crumbs
Garlic powder
Salt and pepper

Peel and slice the eggplant (1/4- to 1/2-inch thick) and place in a single layer on an oiled, ridged cookie sheet. Spray the tops of the eggplant slices with the olive oil. Season with salt, pepper, and garlic powder. Broil 3–5 minutes on each side.

In a heavy saucepan, heat the crushed tomatoes on medium-high heat. Add salt, pepper, and garlic. Cook for 30 minutes, stirring occasionally.

To assemble, begin by placing the eggplant in a single layer on the bottom of a 13x9-inch baking pan. Add a thin layer of sauce, cover with bread crumbs, sprinkle with a layer of Parmesan and mozzarella cheeses. Continue to layer in this manner, creating 3 to 4 layers. Reserve room at the top of the pan as the dish will expand when cooking. Bake at 350 degrees for 45 minutes. Remove and let set for 15 minutes.

Serves 4–6

Savor THE FARM
VEGETABLES AND SIDE DISHES

AGLIO E OLIO E ALICHIE
GARLIC WITH OLIVE OIL AND ANCHOVIES

by John O'Connor, Proprietor, The Atlantic Café

1 lb. capellini pasta or thin spaghetti
3–4 cans flat anchovies in olive oil
1 cup olive oil
1/4 lb. Romano cheese, finely grated
Fresh Italian parsley, chopped
Pepper
Water

In a heavy saucepan, bring 1 cup olive oil and 2 cups water to a boil. Reduce heat, add anchovies, and return to a boil. Cook over medium-high heat until anchovies dissolve, 10 minutes.

While anchovies are cooking, boil the water for the pasta. Drop the pasta into the water when the anchovies are almost done. Follow package directions for cooking. This will be quick as it is a fast-cooking pasta. Drain pasta.

In a large bowl, add the cooked pasta and pour the anchovy sauce on top. Add Romano cheese and freshly ground pepper. Toss until pasta is coated. The thin sauce will drain to the bottom of the bowl, so continue to toss while serving. Best when served immediately. Great with crusty bread and Eggplant Parmigiana. Your guests will not believe they are eating anchovies!

PORTOBELLO AND GOAT CHEESE PASTA

1 tbsp. butter
2 tbsp. olive oil
6 medium onions, chopped
1 tsp. salt
1 tsp. sugar
2 lbs. portobello mushrooms
1 tbsp. butter
1 tbsp. olive oil
1/2 tsp. salt
6 tbsp. chopped fresh Italian parsley
Salt and pepper to taste
24 oz. short tube pasta, uncooked
8 oz. soft herbed goat cheese, crumbled
3 tbsp. freshly grated Parmesan cheese
1 tbsp. olive oil

Melt 1 tablespoon butter in 2 tablespoons olive oil in a large skillet. Add the onions, 1 teaspoon salt, and the sugar. Cook over medium heat for 20 to 30 minutes or until the onions are brown, stirring frequently. Remove to a bowl.

Remove stems from the mushrooms. Cut the caps into halves. Cut the halves horizontally, 1/4-inch thick. Melt 1 tablespoon butter in 1 tablespoon olive oil in the skillet. Add the mushrooms and 1/2 teaspoon salt. Cook over medium heat for 8 to 10 minutes or until tender and brown, stirring occasionally. Add the cooked onions and parsley. Season with salt and pepper to taste.

Cook the pasta in boiling salted water in a large saucepan until al dente. Drain the pasta, reserving 2 cups of the water. Place the pasta in a large serving bowl. Add 1 cup of the reserved water, mushroom mixture, goat cheese, Parmesan cheese, and 1 tablespoon olive oil and toss to mix well. Add the remaining reserved water 1/4 cup at a time until the pasta is the desired consistency. Serve immediately with the additional Parmesan cheese.

Note: If the herbed goat cheese is unavailable, use plain goat cheese mixed with 1 clove of garlic, minced, and 1 teaspoon basil.

VEGETARIAN LASAGNA

1 small eggplant, diced
1 large red pepper, diced
1 lb. mushrooms, diced
2 onions, diced
1 lb. spinach
2 small zucchini, thinly sliced, lengthwise
2 cloves garlic
1 (3-lb.) jar, spaghetti sauce
1 lb. block mozzarella cheese, grated
2 lbs. ricotta cheese
1/2 lb. sharp Cheddar cheese, grated
1/4 cup fresh basil, chopped
1 tbsp. oregano
1/2 stick butter
3–4 tbsp. extra-virgin olive oil
1 box lasagne noodles, uncooked
1 can black olives, chopped

Place a large pot on high heat. Add butter and olive oil and allow to melt. Add eggplant, pepper, mushrooms, and onion. Cook until softened, stir occasionally. Add garlic after vegetables are soft. Cook until you can smell it. Add spaghetti sauce, carrots, olives, and basil. Reduce to a simmer and allow flavors to blend. Remove from stove and allow to cool. (Reserve a small amount of sauce and cheese for top.)

Lay one layer of noodles on bottom of a 9x12-inch baking pan. Cover with a layer of spinach, then zucchini. Next put half of the sauce over the layer, half of the ricotta, half of the mozzarella, and half of the Cheddar cheese. Put next layer of noodles on top and repeat. Place one more layer of noodles on top and cover with remaining sauce and cheese.

Bake at 325 degrees for 1 1/2 hours. Let cool 5 minutes to set. Drain excess moisture with a baster. You may need to extend the sides of casserole dish with foil if not using a dish with tall sides.

VODKA TOMATO RIGATONI

2 tbsp. butter
1 small onion, chopped
2 cloves of garlic, minced
1 tbsp. dried Italian seasoning
1 (14- or 16-oz.) can Italian plum tomatoes,
    chopped and juices reserved
3 oz. prosciutto, sliced
1/4 cup vodka, or more to taste
3/4 cup whipping cream
1/2 cup (2 oz.) grated Parmesan cheese
8 oz. rigatoni or other tubular pasta, cooked
    and drained
Salt and pepper to taste
Grated Parmesan cheese

Melt the butter in a heavy skillet over medium-high heat. Add the onion, garlic, and Italian seasonings and sauté for 4 minutes or until the onion is translucent. Add the tomatoes with the reserved juices and prosciutto, and simmer for 10 minutes, stirring occasionally.

Add the vodka and simmer for 5 minutes, stirring occasionally. Add the cream and 1/2 cup Parmesan cheese and simmer for 4 minutes or until slightly thickened, stirring occasionally. Add the pasta and stir to coat with the sauce. Season with salt and pepper. Serve with Parmesan cheese.

Savor

THE SEA

SEAFOOD

MUSSELS WITH PARSLEY AND GARLIC

2 lbs. mussels, cleaned and beards removed
3 cloves garlic, coarsely chopped
1 cup fresh flat-leafed parsley
4 tbsp. unsalted butter, cut into pieces
1/4 tsp. salt
1/4 tsp. freshly ground black pepper

Preheat oven to 450 degrees.

Spread mussels in a 13x9-inch baking dish. Blend all remaining ingredients to a paste in a food processor. Spoon mixture over mussels. Cover tightly with foil and bake in the middle of the oven until all mussels are open, 12 to 15 minutes. Discard any unopened mussels.

CRAB RAMEKIN

1 lb. crabmeat
1/2 cup celery, chopped
1/4 cup green pepper, chopped
1 tbsp. scallions, chopped
1 tbsp. lemon juice
1/2 tsp. salt
1/3 cup mayonnaise
2 tbsp. butter, melted

1 hard-boiled egg, chopped
1 tsp. Dijon mustard
1 tsp. Worcestershire sauce
Dash red pepper
2/3 cup bread crumbs
1 tbsp. cold butter
Lemon slices for garnish (optional)

Preheat oven to 350 degrees. Pick over the crabmeat to remove any cartilage. Combine crab with all the remaining ingredients except the cold butter and bread crumbs. Divide among 4-oz. ramekins and top with bread crumbs (a good-quality white bread sieved through hands). Add a thin slice of butter, achieved by pulling a vegetable peeler across cold butter, and bake for 7 minutes.
Serves 6–8

Savor THE SEA
SEAFOOD

CRAB IMPERIAL

2 cups crab
2 tbsp. chopped onions
1 cup chopped celery
3 tbsp. flour
1/2 tsp. dry mustard
1/2 tsp. salt
1/2 tsp. paprika
Dash cayenne pepper
1/2 tsp. pepper
1 1/2 cup milk
1 tbsp. chili sauce
1/4 cup pimento
2 tsp. parsley
2/3 cup chopped almonds
1 tsp. Worcestershire sauce

Cook onion and celery in butter for 5 minutes. Blend in the flour and the seasonings. Stir in milk slowly; cook until thickened.

Stir in Worcestershire sauce, chili sauce, pimento, and parsley. Blend in crab, topped with chopped almonds, and bake 20–25 minutes at 350 degrees.

SHRIMP WITH CHAMPAGNE BEURRE BLANC

SAUCE:
2 cups Champagne
1/2 cup shallots, chopped
2 tbsp. Champagne vinegar or white wine vinegar
1/2 tsp. whole black peppercorns
2 sticks butter, cut into 16 pieces

SHRIMP:
1 cup Champagne
1/4 cup extra-virgin olive oil
3 tbsp. minced shallot
1/2 tsp. freshly ground black pepper
24 extra large shrimp, peeled, de veined, with tails left intact
1 tbsp. each, minced fresh chives, tarragon, and parsley

To make the sauce, combine all ingredients except butter in a heavy medium-sized saucepan. Boil until reduced to 1/4 cup liquid, about 20 minutes. Sauce can be made up to 4 hours ahead. Cover and leave at room temperature.

To prepare the shrimp, combine all ingredients in a Ziploc bag except for chive, tarragon, and parsley. Let marinate at room temperature 30 minutes to 1 hour. Mix chives, tarragon, and parsley in a small bowl. Preheat broiler. Spray a pan with cooking spray. Drain shrimp. Arrange shrimp on the pan in a single layer, broiling until just opaque in the center, 2 minutes per side. Remove shrimp from the broiler and put in a shallow bowl.

Rewarm sauce base over medium-low heat. Whisk in butter, 1 tablespoon at a time, just allowing each to melt before adding the next one (do not let boil or sauce will break). Season with salt and pepper. Spoon sauce over warm shrimp and sprinkle with fresh herbs before serving. This is a very elegant dish, but easy to prepare. Great as an appetizer, or as a main meal with salad and bread. Serves 7 as an appetizer and 4 as an entrée

STUFFED QHAHOGS

4 dozen quahogs
1 loaf Portuguese bread
3/4 cup minced linguiça
1 stick butter or margarine
4 cloves garlic, minced
4 medium onions, chopped
3/4 to 1 cup mix of red, yellow, and orange peppers, chopped
2 stalks celery, chopped
4 tbsp. fresh parsley, chopped
1/2 cup white wine
Salt and pepper, to taste

Open quahogs, saving all juice. Chop clams in a blender or food processor and set aside. Melt the butter in a deep pan or skillet. Sauté onion, peppers, garlic, and celery until soft. Add parsley and linguiça, stirring, and cook for a few minutes. Add wine and clam meats. Cook 5 minutes longer. Break bread into small pieces (you can use a food processor). Wet with reserved clam juice. Soak well. Knead until a paste forms and there are no lumps. If you need more liquid, add more wine. Add bread crumbs to skillet mixture and mix well. Add salt and pepper. Stuff quahog shells full. Place on cookie sheets in a single layer and freeze until ready to eat.

To serve, bake in a 350-degree oven for 30–40 minutes.

SCALLOPS ITALIANO

1 clove garlic
1 tbsp. butter
1 large tomato
Juice of 1/2 a lemon
Pinch of parsley
Pinch of oregano
Pinch of salt and pepper
1/4 cup white wine
Pinch of crushed red pepper
1/2 lb. fresh scallops
1/2 pkg. angel hair pasta (for 2 people)
Parmesan cheese
Lemon wedges

Sauté garlic in a large pan with butter. Add chopped tomato, lemon juice, all the spices, and the white wine. Cover and "simmer down" until it reduces by two-thirds. Meanwhile, cook the pasta according to package directions.

Sprinkle the scallops over the mixture in the sauté pan, cover and simmer for 3 minutes.

Pour the scallop mixture over pasta on individual plates. Sprinkle with fresh grated Parmesan cheese and serve with a lemon wedge. Garlic toast and a glass of white wine complete the meal. Serves 2

LOBSTER DE JONGHE

24 oz. lobster meat, cooked and cubed
1/2 cup bread crumbs
2 tbsp. thinly sliced green onions
1/2 cup grated Parmesan cheese
1/4 cup melted butter
1 tbsp. lemon juice
1/2 cup butter, melted

Preheat oven to 350 degrees. In a small bowl, mix together bread crumbs, green onions, Parmesan cheese, 1/4 cup melted butter, and lemon juice. Set aside.

Place lobster meat into 6 ramekins. Pour 1/2 cup melted butter over lobster and top with bread crumb mixture. Bake for 25 minutes, or until topping is browned.

COMPANY SHRIMP

1 pint cherry tomatoes, quartered
2 tbsp. fresh dill, chopped
1 tsp. extra-virgin olive oil
1 tsp. minced garlic
1/2 tsp. salt
1/4 tsp. pepper
8 oz. orzo pasta, cooked and drained
1 (10-oz.) pkg. spinach, chopped, thawed, squeezed dry
10 oz. shrimp, cooked and peeled
1/2 cup feta cheese, crumbled
1 tbsp. grated Parmesan cheese

Combine tomatoes, dill, oil, garlic, salt, and pepper in a large bowl. Let stand 10 minutes. Stir in orzo, and then add remaining ingredients. Spoon into a shallow 1 1/2-quart microwave-safe casserole. Cover and microwave on high for 5 minutes or until heated through.

BAKED SHRIMP IN LEMONY GARLIC SAUCE

1 1/4 lb. large shrimp, peeled and deveined
Cooking spray
1/4 cup fresh lemon juice
2 tbsp. light butter, melted
3 cloves garlic, minced
1 tsp. Worcestershire sauce
3/4 tsp. lemon-pepper seasoning
1/4 tsp. ground red pepper
2 tbsp. chopped fresh parsley

Preheat oven to 425 degrees.

Arrange shrimp in a single layer in 13x9x2-inch baking dish coated with cooking spray. Combine lemon juice and next 5 ingredients; pour over shrimp. Bake for 8 to 10 minutes or until shrimp are done. Sprinkle with parsley.

BAKED STUFFED SHRIMP

24 jumbo shrimp
1 medium onion, minced
1 green pepper, minced
2 tbsp. butter
1 can flaked crabmeat
1 tsp. sherry
1 tsp. dry mustard
1 tsp. Worcestershire sauce
1/2 tsp. salt
2 tbsp. mayonnaise

Split 24 cooked, cleaned jumbo shrimp and open flat. Cook a medium-sized minced onion and a minced green pepper in 2 tbsp. butter, until soft, but not brown. Add can of flaked crabmeat, sherry, dry mustard, Worcestershire sauce, salt, and mayonnaise. Mix well.

Stuff shrimp with crabmeat mixture. Dot with 2 tbsp. butter and sprinkle lightly with Parmesan cheese, and paprika. Bake at 350 degrees for 10 minutes.

Savor THE SEA
SEAFOOD

COQUILLES SAINT-JACQUES

4 tbsp. butter
1/2 cup finely chopped Vidalia or other sweet onion (1 small)
1/3 cup tomatoes, peeled, seeded, and diced
4 oz. baby portobello mushrooms, sliced
2 lbs. sea scallops
1/2 cup dry white wine
2 tbsp. unbleached all-purpose flour
3/4 to 1 cup cream, half-and-half, or milk
3 to 4 tbsp. freshly grated Parmesan cheese
Salt
Freshly ground black pepper
Cayenne pepper
1 tbsp. chopped fresh parsley

Preheat the oven to 400 degrees. Heat 1 tablespoon of the butter in a large nonreactive skillet. Add the onions and cook, stirring occasionally, for 2 minutes. Stir in the tomatoes and mushrooms and cook for 3 minutes longer. Halve the scallops, and add to the pan along with the wine. Cover the pan, lower the heat, and simmer for about 2 minutes. Remove from the heat and set aside.

In a small saucepan, heat 2 tablespoons of the butter. Remove from the heat, stir in the flour, then put back on the stove and cook over low heat for 2 minutes. Remove the pan from the heat. Heat the cream and add it to the flour mixture. Stir, return the pan to the heat, and cook over medium-low until sauce is thickened. Stir the cream mixture into the scallops and vegetables and add 2 tablespoons of the cheese. Taste and season with salt, black pepper, and cayenne pepper.

Spoon the mixture into a buttered baking dish, sprinkle with the remaining cheese, dot with the remaining butter, and bake for 10 to 15 minutes, or until the top is browned. Or, you can brown the top under the broiler. Sprinkle with parsley before serving. Serves 4

Savor THE SEA
SEAFOOD

LINGUIÇA SAUSAGE WITH LITTLENECK CLAMS

by Chef Dante Benatti, The Atlantic Café

3 tbsp. olive oil
1 yellow onion, finely chopped
1 red or green bell pepper, seeded and diced
1/4 tsp. coarse salt
Pinch of red pepper flakes (optional)
2 or 3 cloves garlic, minced
1 tsp. sweet paprika
1 lb. linguiça or other smoked pork sausage such as kielbasa,
      sliced 3/4-inch thick
1/2 cup dry white wine
1 (28-oz.) can plum tomatoes, drained and chopped
24 littleneck clams, about 2 lbs., well scrubbed
2 tbsp. chopped flat-leaf Italian parsley

In a wide saucepan or large, deep frying pan, warm the olive oil over medium-low heat. Add the onion, bell pepper, coarse salt, and red pepper flakes (if using) and cook, stirring often, until soft, about 15 minutes. Add the garlic and paprika and cook, stirring, for about 1 minute longer. Stir in the sausage and cook, stirring occasionally, until heated through, 2–3 minutes.

Raise the heat to high. Add the wine and tomatoes. Bring to a simmer and cook for 5 minutes to blend the flavors. Discard any clams that are gaping and do not close when tapped. Add the clams, cover, and cook until the clams open, which will take 6–10 minutes. The clams may not all open at the same time. As they do open, scoop them out with a slotted spoon, and set them aside in a large bowl. After 10 minutes, scoop out and discard any clams that failed to open.

Return the cooked clams, still in their shells, to the pan. Spoon into warmed pasta bowls and sprinkle with the chopped parsley. Serve immediately. Serves 4

POLENTA-CRUSTED SWORDFISH WITH A BLACK BEAN, AVOCADO, TOMATO AND FRESH CORN SALSA

by Chef All Kovalencik, Company of the Cauldron

3-1/2 lbs. swordfish, cut 2-inches thick
1 cup polenta or yellow cornmeal
2 whole avocados, pitted and diced
1 small red onion, finely chopped
1 tsp. ground cumin
1/2 teaspoon ground coriander
1/2 teaspoon garlic powder
1/2 teaspoon onion powder
1 jalapeño pepper, finely diced
1/4 cup olive oil
5 whole key limes, zested and juiced
1 bunch cilantro, finely chopped
1tbsp. rice wine vinegar
3 ears fresh corn, stripped from cob
1/2 cup black beans, cooked in rich chicken stock
2 whole tomatoes, seeded and chopped
1 tablespoon brown sugar
1 bunch scallions, chopped

Cut swordfish into six two-inch pieces. Combine 1/2 of the spices with all the polenta in mixing bowl with salt and pepper. Rub swordfish with a little olive oil and dredge in polenta mixture.

Mix the black beans, tomatoes, chopped avocados, red onion, cilantro, jalapeño, lime juice and zests, half the olive oil, and the rest of the spices. Add salt, pepper, brown sugar, and rice wine vinegar to taste and set aside.

Pan sear swordfish at medium-high heat in olive oil for two minutes on each side. Place on rack in a hot oven at 400 degrees until just cooked through, 5 to 10 minutes.

Serve swordfish over mashed potatoes. Top with salsa and garnish with fried sage leaf.

FINNAN HADDIE

2 lbs. smoked haddock fillets
4 tbsp. butter
3 tbsp. flour
2 cups milk
2 cups heavy cream

Melt butter in a sauce pan. While stirring, add flour to butter on medium-low heat. This makes a roux. Add milk and cream slowly while stirring. Add haddock and simmer while stirring. Pepper to taste. The longer it simmers, the smokier the flavor. If it gets too thick, add more milk. Serve over rice or toast. Serves 4

Note: Smoked cod can be substituted for the smoked haddock.

SALMON CROQUETTES

3 cups fresh salmon, chopped
1 cup light cream
2 tbsp. butter
1 tbsp.flour
1/2 tsp. vinegar
1 egg, well beaten
Salt and pepper
Fat for frying
Flour for dredging
Egg wash
Dry bread crumbs

Make a white sauce with the butter, flour, and cream. Cook and beat until smooth and creamy. Add salmon and vinegar and season with salt and pepper to taste. Just before removing from heat, add the egg. Spread the mixture on a well-buttered plate.

When quite cool, roll into small croquettes. Dip into egg wash, roll in flour and then in the bread crumbs. Deep fry at 375 degrees until golden brown. Drain well and serve hot.

Savor THE SEA
SEAFOOD

BBQ ROASTED SALMON

1/2 cup pineapple juice
2 tbsp. fresh lemon juice
4 (6-oz.) salmon fillets

RUB:
2 tbsp. brown sugar
4 tsp. chili powder
2 tsp. grated lemon rind
3/4 tsp. cumin
1/2 tsp. salt
1/4 tsp. cinnamon
Cooking spray

Combine pineapple juice, lemon juice, and salmon in a plastic bag. Seal and marinate one hour, turning occasionally.

Preheat oven to 400 degrees. Remove salmon from bag and discard marinade.

Combine dry ingredients in a bowl to make the rub. Spray an 11x7-inch baking dish. Place fillets in dish and cover with rub mix. Bake 14 minutes, or until salmon easily flakes. Serve with lemon. Serves 4

BOUILLABAISSE

1 cup chopped onion
1/4 cup diced carrot
1 clove garlic, minced
1/2 cup oil (olive or salad)
3 lbs. fish (cod, sole, or other), cut into 3-inch pieces
1 lb. lobster meat, cut into pieces
1 (16 oz.) can tomatoes
2 bay leaves
2 quarts water
1 lb. raw shrimp, cleaned
2 lbs. little necks
2 lbs. mussels, cleaned
1 (10 1/2 oz.) can condensed chicken or beef broth
1/2 cup chopped pimento
1/4 cup fresh parsley
1 tbsp. salt
1/2 tsp. saffron
Pepper to taste

In a large kettle, cook and stir onion, carrot, and garlic
in oil until onion is tender. Add fish, lobster, tomato (with
liquid), bay leaves, and water.   Heat to boiling and
then reduce heat. Cover and simmer 15 minutes. Add
clams, mussels, and the rest of the ingredients. Simmer
15 minutes or until shells open. Serve with French bread.
Serves 4

Savor THE SEA
SEAFOOD

BAKED CODFISH LOAF

1 cup milk
1 cup soft bread crumbs
2 cups codfish, cooked and flaked
Grated rind of half a lemon
1 tsp. salt
1/4 tsp. pepper
2 tbsp. butter
2 eggs

SAUCE:
3 tbsp. butter
3 tbsp. flour
1/2 tsp. salt
Paprika
1 1/2 cups milk
1 cup fresh shrimp, cleaned and shredded
1 tbsp. capers

Scald the milk; pour it onto the bread and set aside until crumbs absorb most of the milk. Combine with the flaked fish, lemon rind, salt, pepper, and butter. Fold in the eggs, well beaten. Transfer to an oiled bread pan; place in a pan of water and bake in a moderate oven (350 degrees) for 45 minutes or until the loaf is firm. Cool slightly, unmold, and serve with hot shrimp sauce.

To prepare the sauce: Melt the butter. Add the flour, salt, and paprika. Mix to a smooth paste. Gradually add the milk. Cook and stir until mixture thickens. Add the shrimp and capers. Heat to boiling point and serve.

Savor THE SEA
SEAFOOD

BAKED SCROD

1 lb. scrod, or other white fish
1 to 2 tbsp. lemon juice
2 to 4 tbsp. butter, melted
1/2 tsp. oregano
1/2 tsp. thyme
Dash of pepper
10 to15 Ritz crackers
1 clove garlic, minced

Crush the crackers. Add to melted butter and garlic. Mix in spices.
Place fish in greased or sprayed baking dish. Sprinkle lemon juice over
fish. Top fish with cracker crumb mixture. Bake at 350–400 degrees
until done. About 10–15 minutes depending on thickness of fish.

FLOUNDER PARMESAN

4 flounder fillets
Salt
Pepper
Flour
2 eggs, beaten
Fine bread crumbs
1/2 cup grated Parmesan cheese
Paprika
Salt
Cayenne
1 tbsp. chopped parsley
1/2 tsp. oregano
3 tbsp. butter or oil

Wash and wipe fillets. Season with salt and pepper. Dust with flour
and dip in egg. Mix crumbs, cheese, and seasonings. Dip fish in
crumbs and coat well. Let stand for 15 minutes (or refrigerate). Brown
well in melted, frothy oil or butter on both sides. Sprinkle with chopped
parsley and oregano.

NORTH ATLANTIC SALMON PASTA

by Chef John Hentshel, Turtle's Restaurant, Siesta Key, FL

8 oz. cubed salmon
Pinch of white pepper
1 tsp. roasted garlic
3 oz. Champagne
2 oz. heavy cream
1 oz. fresh Parmesan cheese
4 oz. fresh spinach, finely chopped
8 oz. cooked linguini

This dish moves along very quickly. Total cooking time should be 3 minutes. Have all your ingredients ready to go before you start.

Prepare linguini according to package directions. Sauté cubed salmon in olive oil until translucent. Add white pepper and roasted garlic. Deglaze the pan with Champagne and add heavy cream, Parmesan cheese and spinach. Sauté for 1 minute. Toss with linguini and serve.

ROASTED STRIPED BASS

4 skinless bass fillets
1/2 cup extra-virgin olive oil
Salt and pepper
4 cloves garlic, thinly sliced
1 1/2 pints cherry tomatoes, halved
1/4 tbsp. Kalamata olives, halved and pitted
3 tbsp. capers, drained
2 tsp. oregano, finely chopped

Heat oven to 400 degrees with rack in the center. Rub both sides of fish with 2 tablespoons olive oil. Season with salt and pepper. Heat remaining 2 tbsp. oil in a medium skillet over medium heat. Add garlic and cook. Add olives, capers, and oregano. Spoon mixture over fish and transfer to oven. Cook fish until opaque, 10 to 15 minutes. Serve immediately.

Savor THE SEA
SEAFOOD

FRESH TUNA NIÇOISE

4 tuna steaks
2 tbsp. olive oil
8 sprigs fresh thyme
Freshly ground black pepper
4 tbsp. finely chopped scallions
2 tbsp. finely chopped pimento-stuffed green olives
2 tbsp. finely chopped capers, drained
4 tbsp. balsamic vinegar
Freshly ground black pepper to taste
2 tsp. anchovy paste
2/3 cup olive oil
4 tbsp. chopped fresh parsley

Coat tuna fish with olive oil, thyme, and pepper. Set aside for 15
minutes. Put scallions, olives, and capers in a mixing bowl. Stir in vinegar
and pepper. Beat in anchovy paste and oil. Just before serving stir
in parsley. Grill tuna fish on a barbecue or broil in the oven for 3 to 4
minutes a side. Spoon over the sauce. Serves 4

STUFFED BAKED BLUEFISH

3 tbsp. butter
1 cup chopped celery
1/2 cup chopped fresh tomatoes
1 clove garlic, minced
2 leeks, chopped
1/4 cup chopped green pepper
Salt and freshly ground black pepper, to taste
1 (4-lb.) bluefish, boned, whole or filleted
2 limes

Melt butter in a skillet. Add all ingredients, except fish and limes, and
sauté until vegetables are tender and lightly browned, about 10 minutes.
Place fish in a greased baking dish. Spoon sautéed vegetables into
cavity of fish, or on top of one fillet, covering with the other. Sprinkle
fish with salt and pepper. Cover dish with foil and seal. (May be done
ahead to this point and refrigerated several hours until ready to bake.)
Preheat oven to 350 degrees. Bake fish 1 hour. Remove foil for last 10
minutes to brown fish. Serve with lime wedges.

Savor THE SEA
SEAFOOD

LEMONADE SOLE

1 lb. fillet of sole, flounder or other mild white fish
1 tbsp. butter, melted
3 tbsp. lemonade concentrate, thawed
2 tbsp. fresh parsley, chopped
Salt to taste
1/8 tsp. white pepper
1/2 tsp. tarragon
2 tbsp. finely chopped green onion
1/2 cup sour cream or mayonnaise
3 tbsp. Parmesan cheese
Paprika
White pepper

Preheat oven to 350 degrees. Using a pastry brush, grease a baking dish or au gratin dish with melted butter. Place fillets in dish; brush with butter, then spoon lemonade concentrate evenly over fish. Cook 8 to 10 minutes, watching carefully until fish flakes easily. Meanwhile, combine next seven ingredients. Preheat broiler. Spread sour cream mixture over fillets; place under broiler until golden brown. Sprinkle with paprika and pepper. Good served with tiny pearl onions, French bread, and white wine.

CLAMBAKE IN A POT

1 lb. linguiça
3 lbs. mussels, cleaned and debearded
4 (1 1/2-lb.) lobsters
4 ears of corn, husked
1 can of beer or 1/2 cup water
3 lbs. littleneck clams
1 1/2 lbs. red or new potatoes
1 lb. bacon

Optional spices: bay leaf, garlic, basil, and oregano

Put linguiça and bacon in the bottom of a large steamer pot. Add clams and mussels. Top with potatoes. Sprinkle in the spices. Top with the corn and lobsters. Add the beer or water (1/2 cup).

Cover and cook on high for 15 minutes, shaking the pot every few minutes. After 15 minutes, check potatoes. When potatoes are done, scoop out the lobsters and corn and set aside. Scoop out the rest of the ingredients to four platters. Arrange the lobster, and corn around the edge of the platter. Serve with melted butter. Serves 4

Savor

THE TRADITIONS

MEAT AND POULTRY

THREE WIVES' MEATLOAF

2 lb. hamburger
Salt and pepper
3/4 cup Quaker Oats
1 cup evaporated milk
2 tbsp. onions, diced

SAUCE:
2 tbsp. Worcestershire sauce
2 tbsp. brown sugar
4 tbsp. onion, diced
2 tbsp. balsamic vinegar
1 cup ketchup

Mix meat, oats, 2 tablespoons diced onion and evaporated milk together. Season with salt and pepper. Combine the remaining ingredients to make the sauce. Spoon on top of loaf. Bake at 350 degrees for 1 hour. Serve with mashed potatoes and peas.

Savor THE TRADITIONS
MEAT AND POULTRY

BEEF AND SOUR CREAM CASSEROLE

2 lb. chuck, cut in cubes
1 clove garlic, minced
6 scallions, sliced
6 tbsp. butter
1 cup sour cream
3 fresh tomatoes, peeled and chopped
2 tsp. Worcestershire sauce

1 tsp. salt
1/4 tsp. pepper
1/4 tsp. dill
Dash of Tabasco
3 tbsp. flour
1/2 cup red wine

Sauté beef in butter with garlic and scallions. Add all ingredients except flour and red wine. Place in covered casserole and bake at 350 degrees for 1 1/2 hours. Mix red wine and flour, add to casserole and bake 20 minutes. Serve over noodles.

BEEF BRISKET

1 (4- to 5-lb.) fresh beef brisket
1 cup ketchup or chili sauce
1/4 cup chopped onion
1 tbsp. prepared mustard
1/4 tsp. freshly ground pepper

2 tbsp. apple cider vinegar
1 tbsp. prepared horseradish
2 tsp. salt
1 tbsp. cornstarch
2 tbsp. cold water

Trim the excess fat from the brisket. Place in a shallow baking pan. Mix the ketchup, onion, prepared mustard, pepper, vinegar, and horseradish in a bowl. Pour over the brisket. Marinate, covered, in the refrigerator for 3 to 12 hours. Sprinkle with salt. Cover tightly with foil. Bake at 300 degrees for 4 to 5 hours (1 hour per pound) or until tender. Remove the brisket to a serving platter. Cut into thin slices. Skim the fat from the pan drippings. Thicken the drippings slightly with a mixture of cornstarch and water, if needed. Serve with the brisket. Serves 6 to 8

DINNER PARTY BEEF TENDERLOIN

1 (750 ml) bottle tawny port
2 (750 ml) bottles dry red wine
4 cups beef broth
1/4 cup (1/2 stick) butter
1 2/3 lbs. onions, chopped
6 tbsp. chopped fresh thyme
2 tbsp. butter
2 lbs. mushrooms, sliced
2 tbsp. all-purpose flour
2 tbsp. olive oil
2 (2- to 2 1/4 lb.) beef tenderloins, trimmed
Salt and pepper to taste

Boil the port, wine, and broth in a large stockpot for 35 to 40 minutes or until reduced to 6 cups.

Melt 1/4 cup butter in a large skillet over medium-high heat. Add the onions. Sauté for 15 to 20 minutes or until tender. Add the thyme. Sauté for 10 minutes or until the onions are brown. Remove to a bowl. Melt 2 tablespoons butter in the skillet. Add the mushrooms. Sauté for 15 to 20 minutes or until tender. Return the onions to the skillet. Add the flour. Cook for 3 minutes, stirring constantly. Add to the wine mixture. Simmer over medium heat for 1 hour or until thickened and reduced to 6 cups. You may prepare up to this point and store, covered, in the refrigerator for 24 hours.

Rub the olive oil over the beef. Season with salt and pepper to taste. Arrange on a rack in a roasting pan. Insert a meat thermometer into the thickest portion. Bake at 400 degrees until the meat thermometer registers 125 degrees. Remove from the oven. Let stand for 10 minutes.

Drain the juices from the roast and add to the sauce. Cook until heated through. Cut the beef cross-grain into 1/2-inch slices. Arrange the beef in overlapping slices on a serving platter. Spoon some of the sauce down the center. Serve with the remaining sauce. Serves 10–12

BEEF BOURGUIGNON

1/2 lb. sliced mushrooms
1/4 cup butter
3 slices bacon
2 lb. boneless beef, cut into 2-inch cubes
2 tbsp. flour
1 tbsp. sugar
1/4 tsp. salt
1/4 tsp. thyme
1 bay leaf (remove before serving)
1 peppercorn
3/4 cup beef stock or broth
1 1/2 cup good-quality red wine
1/2 oz. whole small white onions
Cherry tomatoes

In a large Dutch oven, sauté mushrooms in butter. Remove mushrooms and liquid, set aside. Fry bacon until crisp. Remove bacon, cut it up, and set aside. Add cubed beef to the bacon drippings and brown well. Blend in flour, then add sugar, salt, thyme, bay leaf, and peppercorn. Add beef stock, or broth, and red wine (using a good, drinkable wine makes any good dish even better).

Cover and simmer for 1 hour, stirring occasionally. Add whole onions, mushrooms, and bacon. Simmer 1 hour longer. Add more wine and beef stock if liquid has evaporated. Garnish with cherry tomatoes and serve over noodles, rice, or mashed potatoes.

PHIL'S NANTUCKET WINTER-WIND CHILI

1 lb. lean ground beef or turkey (diced works even better)
1 pkg. McCormick (or other brand) chili seasoning mix (any flavor)
1 (14 1/2 oz.) can diced tomatoes
1 (8 oz.) can tomato sauce
1 (15 1/2 oz.) can red beans (frijoles rojos)
1/2 medium onion, diced
3–4 bay leaves

Brown meat in large skillet on medium-high heat. Drain fat.

Stir in diced tomatoes, tomato sauce, seasoning mix, onion, bay leaves, and beans. Bring to a boil, cover. Stir when needed.

Reduce heat and simmer for 10–20 minutes. Chili gets better as it simmers. Stir when needed. Add water as needed. Hotter? Add chili powder to taste. Serve with crackers. If desired, top with shredded cheese and/or sour cream. Double everything for 8 servings.

IRISH GUINNESS BEEF STEW

by Chef Hector Rivas, Kitty Murtagh's Irish Pub and Restaurant

1/4 cup olive oil
1 1/4 lb. stewing beef, cut into 1-inch pieces
6 cloves garlic
6 cups beef stock
2 cups Guinness beer
2 tbsp. tomato paste
1 tbsp. sugar
1 tbsp. Worcestershire sauce
2 bay leaves
2 tbsp. butter
3 lbs. russet potatoes, cut into 1/2-inch pieces (7 cups)
1 large onion, chopped
2 cups diced carrots
Salt and pepper to taste
2 tbsp. chopped fresh parsley

Heat olive oil in a large, heavy pot over medium-high heat. Add beef and sauté until brown on all sides, about 5 minutes. Add garlic and sauté 1 minute. Add beef stock, Guinness beer, tomato paste, sugar, Worcestershire sauce, and bay leaves. Stir to combine. Bring mixture to boil. Reduce heat to medium-low, then cover and simmer 1 hour, stirring occasionally.

While the meat and stock are simmering, melt butter in another large pot over medium heat. Add potatoes, onion, and carrots. Sauté vegetables until golden, about 20 minutes.

Add vegetables to beef stew. Simmer uncovered until vegetables and beef are very tender, about 40 minutes. Discard bay leaves. Tilt pan and spoon off fat. Transfer stew to serving bowls. Sprinkle with parsley and serve. This recipe can be prepared up to 2 days ahead. Salt and pepper to taste. Cool slightly. Refrigerate uncovered until cold, then cover and refrigerate. Bring to simmer before serving. Serves 4–6

BRANDIED PORK CHOPS

8 pork chops
1 tbsp. butter
5 Granny Smith apples, sliced
1/2 cup golden raisins
1 cup chopped pecans

1/2 cup dried apricots, chopped
1/2 cup honey
1/2 tsp. cinnamon
1/2 cup brandy
1/4 cup water

Brown the pork chops in the butter in a skillet. Combine the sliced unpeeled apples, raisins, pecans, apricots, honey, and cinnamon in a bowl and toss to mix well. Layer 1/2 of the apple mixture in a buttered 4-quart baking dish. Arrange the pork chops over the apple mixture. Top with the remaining apple mixture. Sprinkle with a mixture of the brandy and water. Bake, covered, at 350 degrees for 1 hour or until the pork chops are cooked through.

PORK TENDERLOIN WITH ONION AND APPLE CREAM

6 tbsp. whipping cream
2 tbsp. cream sherry
1 tsp. Dijon mustard
1/2 tsp. prepared horseradish
1/2 tsp. salt

1 (12-oz.) whole pork tenderloin
2 tbsp. butter
1 large onion, thinly sliced
1 small apple, thinly sliced

Combine the whipping cream, sherry, Dijon mustard, horseradish, and salt in a small bowl and stir to mix well. Arrange the pork on a rack in a roasting pan. Insert a meat thermometer into the thickest portion. Bake at 425 degrees for 25 to 30 minutes or until the meat thermometer registers 170 degrees, basting frequently with some of the cream mixture.

Melt the butter in a large skillet over medium heat. Add the onion and apple. Cook for 20 minutes or until limp and golden brown, stirring frequently. Add the remaining cream mixture. Bring to a boil. Spoon into a small bowl and keep warm.

Arrange the pork on a small serving platter. Garnish with sprigs of fresh parsley. Serve with the onion and apple cream.

ORANGE DIJON PORK MEDALLIONS

2 tbsp. olive oil
1 1/2 lbs. pork tenderloin
Pepper to taste
1/2 cup white wine or apple juice

3 tbsp. orange marmalade
1 tbsp. Dijon mustard
1 tbsp. butter

Heat the olive oil in a deep 12-inch nonstick skillet over medium heat. Sprinkle the pork lightly with pepper. Cut the pork into slices 1/4-inch thick. Some pieces will be very small. Add the pork to the skillet. Increase the heat to medium-high. Fry for 5 minutes on each side or until cooked through. Remove the pork to a platter and keep warm.

Return the skillet to medium heat. Add the wine, stirring to deglaze the skillet. Cook for 1 minute, stirring constantly. Add the marmalade and Dijon mustard and mix well. Remove from the heat. Add the butter and mix well. Drizzle over the pork. Serves 4

HAM DI PARMA

1/3 cup butter
6 oz. fresh mushrooms, sliced
2 tbsp. grated onion
1/4 cup all-purpose flour
1/4 tsp. oregano
1/8 tsp. pepper
2 cups whipping cream

1 lb. cooked ham, cut into strips
3/4 cup dry white wine, or liquid of choice
1/3 cup sliced green olives or
    pimento-stuffed olives
1 pimento, cut into strips
8 oz. spaghetti, cooked and drained
1/2 cup shredded or grated Parmesan

Melt butter in a large skillet and add the mushrooms and onion. Cook for 5 minutes, stirring occasionally. Remove the mushroom mixture to a platter using a slotted spoon, reserving the pan drippings. Blend the flour, oregano, and pepper into the reserved pan drippings. Add the cream gradually, stirring constantly. Bring to a boil and boil for 1 minute. Stir in the ham, wine, olives, and pimento.

Preheat the broiler. Toss the pasta with 1/4 cup of the cheese in a bowl. Spread in a 2 1/2-quart baking dish or 10x15-inch baking pan with 2-inch sides. Spoon the ham mixture over the pasta and sprinkle with remaining 1/4 cup of cheese. Broil 4 to 6 inches from the heat source until light brown and heated through. You can freeze for future use.

HERB-CRUSTED RACK OF LAMB

by the Caron brothers, Father Paul and Chef David Caron

1 rack of lamb, frenched* and defatted
Salt and freshly cracked pepper
Granulated garlic or garlic powder
Olive oil
2 tbsp. Dijon mustard
1/4 cup seasoned bread crumbs
1 tbsp. fresh rosemary, finely chopped
1 tbsp. fresh thyme, finely chopped

Preheat oven to 375 degrees. Mix together salt, cracked pepper, granulated garlic, chopped rosemary, and chopped thyme. Rub liberally over lamb's exterior. This can be done ahead of time and will enhance the flavor. Refrigerate if not continuing at this point.

Heat a large cast-iron skillet that has been lightly seasoned with olive oil. When the oil begins to smoke, place lamb rack in the pan with the rib bones curling up. Lightly brown and turn until evenly seared on all surfaces. Place entire pan in the preheated oven for 5 minutes. Remove from the oven and baste lamb rack with Dijon mustard. Dust generously with bread crumbs. Return to oven for 10 minutes or until internal temperature registers 135 degrees for medium rare, longer if you prefer it more well done. Remove from the oven and let rest 5 minutes before serving. Serves 2

The term "frenched" refers to the removal of excess fat and silver skin on the top portion of the rib bones. It makes for a nicer presentation and reduces grease and splatter in the oven.

GRILLED LAMB CHOPS WITH MERLOT MARINADE

1 small onion, finely chopped
3 cloves garlic, finely chopped
2 sprigs fresh rosemary,
    coarsely chopped

12 sage leaves, crushed
3/4 cup merlot
1/4 cup olive oil
8 lamb chops

Combine the onion, garlic, rosemary, sage, wine, and olive oil in a noncorrosive bowl and mix well. Add the lamb chops. Marinate, covered, in the refrigerator for 8 to 12 hours. Drain the lamb chops, reserving the marinade. Pour the reserved marinade into a saucepan. Bring to a boil. Boil for 2 to 3 minutes. Arrange the lamb chops on a grill rack. Brush with the cooked marinade. Grill until the lamb chops are cooked through, basting occasionally with the cooked marinade. If sage or rosemary grow in your garden, cut a few sprigs to use as the marinade brush. Serves 4

LAMB GYROS

1 egg
6 cloves garlic, minced
3 tbsp. dried oregano
1 1/2 tsp. salt
1 tsp. pepper
1 lb. ground lamb
1 lb. ground beef
8 gyros (pita)
16 slices of tomato
8 slices sweet onion, halved

TZATZIKI SAUCE:
1 cup plain yogurt
1 cucumber peeled, seeded, and chopped
2 tbsp. lemon juice
2 cloves garlic, minced
1/4 tsp. salt
1/4 tsp. pepper

In a large bowl, combine egg, garlic, oregano, salt, and pepper. Mix with lamb and beef. Pat into a 9x5x3-inch loaf pan. Bake uncovered at 350 degrees for 60–70 minutes, or until no pink remains and a meat thermometer registers 160 degrees. Cool completely and refrigerate for 2 hours.

To make the sauce, combine all the ingredients, cover and refrigerate until serving. Brush pita breads with 1 tablespoon oil, heat on a griddle for one minute. Keep warm. Cut meat loaf into very thin slices. In a large skillet, fry meat loaf slices in remaining oil in batches until crisp. On each pita, layer tomato, onion, meat loaf slices, and Tzatziki sauce. Carefully fold pitas in half. Serve with remaining sauce.

OSSO BUCCO

2 to 3 cloves garlic
2 to 3 onions
2 stalks of celery
2 carrots, peeled
6 tbsp. butter
1/2 cup dry white wine
1 (28-oz.) can Italian crushed tomatoes with added purée
1/2 cup fresh flat-leaf parsley, chopped
Grated rind of 1/2 a lemon
4 to 6 veal shanks, trimmed and tied
Flour
Salt and pepper

Chop garlic cloves, onions, celery stalks, and carrots in food processor and put aside.

Roll veal shanks in flour seasoned with salt and pepper. Melt 6 tablespoons butter in skillet large enough to hold the shanks. Brown the veal shanks turning 1–2 times. Add the vegetable mixture and cook until soft (a few minutes). Add 1/2 cup dry white wine and cook 15 minutes. Add can of Italian crushed tomatoes. Cover and cook on low heat for 2 hours.

At the end of the cooking, remove some marrow from each of the veal shanks. Mix with 1/2 cup fresh chopped parsley and lemon rind. Add to the pan of osso bucco. Keep warm until ready to serve. Serve with risotto and vegetable.

VEAL MARSALA

by Chef Dante Benatti, The Atlantic Café

12 large slices scaloppine of veal
Flour
Olive oil
2 to 3 tbsp. butter
1/2 lb. sliced fresh mushrooms
2 tbsp. chopped chives
2 tbsp. chopped parsley
1 1/2 cups beef broth (or bouillon)
1/2 cup Marsala wine
Paprika
Salt
Pepper

Dust veal slices lightly in flour. Heat 3 to 4 tablespoons olive oil in a skillet. Sauté quickly 3 to 4 slices of veal at a time over high heat until browned. Transfer slices to a casserole and sprinkle each slice with paprika. Add more oil if necessary and repeat process for remaining slices of veal. Melt butter in a skillet. Add mushrooms and sauté for about 5 minutes. Add the chives, parsley, beef broth, and wine. Salt and pepper to taste. Simmer 5 minutes. Pour the sauce over the veal slices in the casserole. Place casserole in a 350-degree oven for 1/2 hour. Serve with buttered noodles.

CHICKEN FRANÇESE

by Chef Thomas Proch, the Club Car

1/2 lb. boneless chicken breasts
Flour for dredging
Salt and freshly ground pepper
2 eggs, beaten
1/2 cup freshly grated Parmesan cheese
1 lemon
1/2 cup dry white wine
4 oz. unsalted butter
1/4 cup olive oil

Cut chicken breasts into roughly six equal pieces. Place the chicken pieces between 2 sheets of waxed paper and pound with a mallet until thin. Season both sides with salt and pepper.

Heat oil and 2 tablespoons butter on medium-high heat in a large sauté pan (large enough to hold the six pieces of chicken). While the butter and oil are heating, beat eggs and cheese well in a wide, shallow dish. Set aside. Place flour in another wide, shallow dish. Dredge the chicken in the flour, then place in the egg and cheese mixture. Set aside on a plate.

Test oil by pinching a piece of flour and egg and dropping it into the oil. If it sizzles and floats, the oil is ready. Gently place the cutlets into the hot oil. Be sure not to brown too quickly. Turn cutlets once until golden brown on both sides, about 1 1/2 minutes.

Remove the cutlets and place on paper towels. Pour out the oil and wipe down the pan. Add remaining butter, swirling in pan until light brown and foamy. Squeeze 1 lemon into the butter, swirling the pan. Add wine, continuing to swirl the pan.

Return cutlets to the pan. Reduce heat to low and simmer for 1 minute. Remove cutlets from pan and place on plates. Pour remaining sauce over cutlets. Serve with rice or pasta. Serves 2

Savor THE TRADITIONS
MEAT AND POULTRY

CHICKEN BREASTS DIANE

4 boneless chicken breast halves
   with fat removed
1/2 tsp. salt
1/4 to1/2 tsp. black pepper
2 tbsp. olive or salad oil
2 tbsp. butter or margarine
3 tbsp. chopped fresh chives, or scallions

Juice of 1/2 a lemon or lime
2 tbsp. brandy or cognac, optional
3 tbsp. parsley, chopped
2 tsp. Dijon-style mustard
1/4 tbsp. chicken broth

Place chicken breast halves between sheets of waxed paper or plastic wrap. Pound slightly with a mallet. Sprinkle with salt and pepper. Heat 1 tbsp. each of oil and butter in a large skillet. Cook chicken over high heat for 4 minutes on each side. Do not cook longer or chicken will be over cooked and dry. Transfer to warm serving platter. Add chives or green onion, lime juice, and brandy, if used, parsley and mustard to the pan. Cook 15 seconds, whisking constantly. Whisk in broth. Stir until sauce is smooth. Whisk in remaining butter and oil. Pour sauce over chicken. Serve immediately. Serve with rice, noodles, mashed or boiled potatoes, and a green vegetable. Serves 4

CHICKEN CLEMENTINE

6 oz. heavy cream
4 to 5 sprigs fresh thyme
2 to 3 tbsp. fresh minced garlic
3 tbsp. olive oil
4 to 6 boneless, skinless chicken breasts

5 oz. white wine
8 oz. crumbled blue cheese
4 oz. unsalted butter, not melted
Flour to coat chicken breasts
Salt and pepper to taste

Coat chicken breasts with flour. Heat olive oil in a sauté pan over moderate heat and cook chicken until golden brown and cooked through. Drain most of the oil from the pan and add garlic and thyme, cooking until garlic is lightly brown and aromatic. Add enough wine to cover bottom of pan about half an inch.

Toss in blue cheese and allow to melt. Add heavy cream and let reduce to your liking. Turn off heat and add whole butter. Shake pan slightly until butter is blended. Adjust salt and pepper to taste. Serve over pasta with a side of fresh vegetables. Serves 4–6

CHICKEN CORDON BLEU

6 boneless, skinless chicken breasts
8 oz. Swiss cheese, sliced
8 oz. cooked ham, sliced
3 tbsp. flour
1 tsp. paprika
6 tbsp. butter
1/2 cup dry white wine
1 cube, or one envelope, chicken bouillon
1 tbsp. cornstarch
1 cup heavy cream

Pound chicken breasts between 2 pieces of waxed paper until thin. Fold cheese and ham to fit on top. Fold breasts over filling and fasten with toothpicks. On waxed paper, mix flour and paprika; use mixture to coat pieces.

Cook chicken in hot butter in a 12-inch skillet over medium heat until browned on all sides. Add wine and bouillon. Reduce heat to low; cover and simmer 30 minutes or until fork tender, remove toothpicks. Set breasts aside to make sauce (keep warm).

In a cup, blend cornstarch and cream until smooth; gradually stir mixture into the skillet. Cook, stirring constantly, until thickened. Serve chicken over rice. Top with the sauce. Serves 6

CHEESE-STUFFED ITALIAN CHICKEN

4 (4-oz.) skinless, boneless chicken breast halves
1/8 tsp. salt
3/4 tsp. dried basil, divided
1/4 tsp. crushed red pepper
1/4 cup minced green bell pepper
4 (3/4-oz.) part-skim mozzarella cheese sticks
2 tbsp. fat-free Italian dressing
1/8 tsp. paprika
1/4 cup dry bread crumbs

Using a mallet, flatten each chicken breast to 1/4-inch thickness between plastic wrap or waxed paper.

Sprinkle chicken evenly with salt, 1/4 tsp. basil, and red pepper. Sprinkle each half with 1 tbsp. bell pepper. Place 1 cheese stick lengthwise down center. Roll up, jelly roll fashion. Brush rolls with Italian dressing. Combine paprika and bread crumbs; dredge chicken rolls in mixture, turning to coat.

Place on a baking sheet coated with cooking spray, seam side down. Lightly coat chicken with spray. Sprinkle with remaining basil. Bake at 400 degrees for 15 minutes or until done. Let stand 2 minutes before serving or until cheese sets.

CHICKEN POT PIE

1/3 cup butter
1/3 cup flour
1/3 cup diced onions
2/3 cup milk
1 3/4 cups chicken broth
Salt and pepper to taste
2 cups diced chicken breast
2 potatoes, diced
2 cups frozen vegetables (corn, peas, carrots, etc.)
1 pkg. prepared pie crust

Set pie crust on counter. Melt butter in a large saucepan. Add flour, onions, salt and pepper. Cook over low heat for 5–10 minutes. In another pan, parboil the potatoes. Drain when tender.

Stir chicken broth and milk into the flour, onion, and butter mixture. Heat to boiling, stirring constantly. Boil for 1 minute, until thickened. Stir in potatoes and vegetables. Pour mixture into the pie crust, cover with top crust and bake for 30–40 minutes at 425 degrees. Let cool for 10 minutes before serving. Serves 6

CHICKEN, SAUSAGE, AND ARTICHOKE HEARTS

1 lb. bulk sausage
3/4 cup flour
1 tsp. dried thyme
Salt and pepper
8 chicken breast halves, cut crosswise
1/3 cup oil
2 cans artichoke hearts
2 envelopes Knorr béarnaise sauce mix
1/3 cup pecans, chopped

Brown and drain sausage and place in a 13x9-inch glass casserole. Mix flour, thyme, salt and pepper and dredge chicken in it. Brown chicken in oil and place over sausage. Drain artichokes (cut in half if too large) and place over chicken. Prepare béarnaise sauce according to package directions, pour over chicken. Top with pecans. Bake at 350 degrees for 1 hour. Serves 8

CHICKEN LIVERS WITH FRESH THYME
AND RASPBERRY VINEGAR

by Chef Thomas Proch, the Club Car

4 tbsp. butter
1 cup onions, finely chopped
Salt and freshly ground pepper to taste
2 tbsp. canola oil
1 lb. chicken livers, split in half, with tough veins removed
1 tbsp. thyme, chopped
1 1/2 tbsp. raspberry vinegar

Melt 2 tbsp. butter in a nonstick saucepan over medium heat. Add the onions. Salt and pepper to taste. Mix thoroughly, then cook, covered, for 10 minutes. The onions should become quite soft.

Heat the oil in a large skillet. When close to smoking, add chicken livers. Season with salt and pepper. Cook over high heat for 1 minute or so, turning over to brown livers on both sides. Remove livers with a slotted spoon and set aside.

Pour excess oil from skillet and wipe down. Add remaining butter to the hot pan. When very hot, add cooked onions and liver. Sprinkle with chopped thyme and deglaze with vinegar, stirring for 2 or 3 minutes. Serve with rice or mashed potatoes, or over mixed greens.

Serves 4

PEANUT CHICKEN

2–3 lb. chicken breast
1/2 cup chunky peanut butter
1/2 cup peanut oil
1/4 cup white wine vinegar
1/4 cup tamari or soy sauce
1/4 cup fresh lemon juice
4 cloves garlic, minced
8 cilantro sprigs, minced
1 whole, dried red chili pepper minced or 1 tsp. dried red pepper flakes
2 tsp. chopped fresh ginger

Mix marinade ingredients together in blender or food processor. Cut boneless skinless chicken breasts into bite-size chunks. Marinate overnight, or at least 1 hour prior to cooking. Put chicken on skewers. Grill until done, approximately 10 minutes. For those on low-sodium diets, use low-sodium soy sauce and no-salt creamy peanut butter. Serves 4–6

WEBSTER CRANBERRY CHICKEN

6 boneless, skinless chicken breasts
1 (8-oz.) can jellied cranberry sauce
1/3 cup soy sauce
1 cup granulated brown sugar
1 tsp. salt
2 tsp. dry mustard

2 tsp. ground ginger
2 cloves garlic, crushed
2 tbsp. lemon juice
2 cups fresh or frozen cranberries
4 tbsp. cornstarch

Preheat oven to 325 degrees. Salt and pepper chicken and brown in cooking spray. Place in a baking dish. Combine remaining ingredients, except fresh cranberries and cornstarch, and heat to dissolve sugar and cranberry sauce. Pour sauce over chicken. Cover and bake for 1 hour. Baste chicken with sauce as needed. Add fresh cranberries and bake an additional 1/2 hour. Remove chicken and keep warm. Mix cornstarch with a small amount of sauce and return to pan. Cook on stove until thickened. Return chicken to sauce and heat through. Serves 6

Savor THE TRADITIONS
MEAT AND POULTRY

DUCK LEG CONFIT

by Chef Thomas Proch, the Club Car

8 duck legs
5 cups duck fat or chicken fat (available from your butcher)
2 to 4 tbsp. rock salt
2 shallots, chopped
2 tsp. cracked peppercorns
2 bay leaves
3 sprigs fresh thyme
2 cloves garlic, chopped
4 cloves garlic, crushed
1/2 tsp. mustard seed

Trim fat away from the duck legs. Place legs in a stainless steel or glass bowl. Add 1 tbsp. of rock salt per pound of duck. Add shallots, peppercorn, bay leaves, thyme and 2 cloves of chopped garlic. Toss all ingredients for a minute or two. Cover with plastic and refrigerate overnight. Remove duck legs from marinade. Rinse well in cold water. Dry legs with a paper towel.

Place rendered fat in a large, heavy-gauge pan. Place on heat and bring up to 190 degrees. Place legs in the hot fat. Cover pan. Return heat to 190 degrees. Add crushed garlic and mustard seeds. Cook until meat pulls easily off the bone, 2–2 1/2 hours. Serve warm or cold. Serves 4–5

SZECHUAN CHICKEN AND NOODLES

2 whole, boneless chicken breasts
1 lb. fresh Chinese noodles, or other thin pasta
1 head of broccoli, cut into flowerettes
6 scallions, sliced

Sauce:
6 cloves garlic, minced
2 tbsp. fresh ginger, minced
1 tbsp. sugar
6 tbsp. low-sodium soy sauce
1/2 cup tahini (ground sesame seeds)
1/2 tbsp. hot chili oil
3 tbsp. oriental sesame oil
3 tbsp. rice vinegar
3 tbsp. white wine

Poach the chicken breasts and shred. Blanch the broccoli until
crunchy and run under cold water to stop cooking. Drain.

Cook the noodles or pasta until al dente. Drain and toss with
2 tablespoons of vegetable oil.

Mix all sauce ingredients into a blender or food processor. Pour sauce
over noodles and toss well. Add shredded chicken, broccoli, and
scallions. Toss again and serve at room temperature. Serves 6–8

Savor
THE SUNSETS
DESSERTS AND SWEETS

MOLASSES SUGAR COOKIES

3/4 cup butter or margarine
1 cup sugar
1/4 cup molasses
1 egg
2 cups flour
2 tsp. baking soda
1 tsp. cinnamon
1/2 tsp. cloves
1/2 tsp. ginger
1/2 tsp. salt

Cream sugar and butter or margarine. Add molasses and egg. Beat well. Sift flour, soda, cinnamon, cloves, ginger, and salt. Add to sugar mixture. Chill. Form 1-inch balls. Roll in granulated sugar. Place on ungreased cookie sheet. Bake at 375 degrees for 8–10 minutes.

CHRUSCHIKI

6 egg yolks
7 tsp. light cream
1 tsp. vanilla
7 tsp. sugar
1/2 tsp. salt
1 cup flour, or a little more as needed
2 tbsp. brandy

In a bowl mix all ingredients with flour. Place on a floured board and knead until smooth and elastic, about 10 minutes. Roll out on a floured board and cut into strips, 2–3-inches long. Slit in center and pull one end through slit to make a bow.

Fry in deep fat about one minute or until golden brown, turning only once. Sprinkle with confectioners' sugar.

CRANBERRY CRUNCH

1 can whole cranberry sauce
1 cup oatmeal
1 cup brown sugar
1/2 cup flour
1/2 cup (1stick) butter or margarine

Cut margarine or butter into the dry ingredients until crumbly. Press 1/2 of mixture into an 8x8-inch pan. Spread cranberry sauce evenly around pan. Sprinkle remainder of crumb mixture on top. Bake at 350 degrees for about 40 minutes. Cut into squares and serve with unsweetened whipped cream.

CRANBERRY CAKE

1 stick plus 6 tbsp. unsalted butter (divided use)
2 cups sugar
2 tbsp. water
1 tsp.cinnamon
4 cups raw cranberries
1 1/2 cups cake flour, sifted
1/2 tsp. salt
1/2 tsp. soda
1/2 cup light brown sugar
2 large eggs
3/4 cup sour cream
1 tsp. vanilla

Preheat oven to 350 degrees. Generously grease a 9-inch springform pan. Wrap pan with foil on outside to prevent leakage. Melt 1 stick butter in a saucepan. Add 1 1/2 cups sugar, water, and cinnamon. Cook until sugar dissolves. Stir in cranberries. Pour into pan and spread evenly.

Sift flour, baking soda, and salt together. Set aside. Mix 6 tbsp. butter, remaining 1/2 cup sugar and brown sugar on medium speed until fluffy. Add eggs, one at a time. Slowly add 1/2 of the flour mixture. Add sour cream and vanilla. Then add the rest of the flour mixture and mix until smooth. Pour into pan. Bake until golden brown, about 45–50 minutes. Set cake on a rack. Cool for 10 minutes. Run knife around edge to loosen cake. Invert on plate. Can be made two days ahead, covered, airtight.

AUNT DORIS'S MELT-IN-YOUR-MOUTH BLUEBERRY CAKE

1 1/2 cups flour
1 tsp. salt
1 tsp. baking powder
1 cup sugar
2 egg whites
1/2 cup shortening
2 egg yolks
1/3 cup milk
1 tsp. vanilla
1 1/2 cups fresh blueberries, floured

Sift together flour, salt, and baking powder. Beat egg whites and set aside. Cream shortening and sugar until light and creamy. Add the egg yolks, well beaten. To this add, alternatively, the milk and flour mixture. Fold in the egg whites and vanilla. Lastly, add the floured blueberries. Pour batter into a 9x9-inch greased and floured pan. Sprinkle lightly with sugar. Bake at 350 degrees for 35–45 minutes.

BLUEBERRY LEMON BUNDT CAKE

2 1/4 cups flour, plus 1 tbsp. for blueberries
1 pkg. lemon pudding or pie-filling mix
2 tsp. baking powder
1/2 tsp.salt
1 cup unsalted butter, at room temperature
1 cup light brown sugar (granulated or packed)
Confectioners' sugar for dusting (optional)

4 eggs
1 tsp. vanilla
1 cup sour cream
2 cups blueberries
2 tbsp. lemon zest, grated

Preheat oven to 350 degrees. Whisk flour, pudding, baking powder, and salt. In a mixing bowl, cream butter and sugars on high speed until fluffy. Add eggs, one at a time, beating until incorporated. Beat in vanilla. Reduce speed to low and add flour mixture in three additions, alternating with two additions of sour cream.

In a bowl, toss blueberries and lemon zest with 1 tbsp. flour and fold into batter. Coat a 12-inch bundt pan with cooking spray. Spread batter in pan. Bake on bottom rack for 60 to 70 minutes. Cool in the pan 20 minutes. Invert onto a rack and cool completely, top side up. Dust with confectioners' sugar, if desired.

APPLE SQUARES

2 cups flour
1 cup sugar
1/2 tsp. baking powder
1/2 tsp. salt
2/3 cup butter
1 egg, beaten
2 tbsp. flour
1 tsp. cinnamon
1 tsp. nutmeg
5 1/2 cups tart apples, peeled, cored, and sliced thin

Combine 2 cups flour, 1/2 cup of the sugar, baking powder, and salt. Cut in cold butter with fork until crumbs form. Stir in egg. Press 1/2 of the mixture into an ungreased 11x7x2-inch pan.

In a large bowl, combine remaining 1/2 cup sugar, 2 tablespoons flour, cinnamon, nutmeg, and apples. Layer apple mixture over crust. Sprinkle with remaining crumbs. Bake at 350 degrees for 45–50 minutes.

INDIAN PUDDING

4 cups milk
1/2 cup sugar
1/2 cup yellow corn meal
3 eggs, slightly beaten
1 tsp. grated orange peel (optional)
1 cup dark molasses
1/2 tsp. cinnamon
1 tsp. ginger
1 tsp. salt
Whipped cream or vanilla ice cream

Scald milk with 1/4 cup sugar. Add cornmeal and continue stirring over low heat until smooth and slightly thickened. Remove from heat and add eggs, orange peel, 1/4 sugar, molasses, and spices. Mix well. Pour into buttered baking dish about 2" deep. Bake 1 hour at 375 degrees. Serve with ice cream or whipped cream.

BANANA FRITTERS

2 egg yolks
2/3 cup milk
1 tbsp. butter, melted
1 cup unbleached flour
1/4 tsp. salt
1 tbsp. sugar
1 tbsp. Grand Marnier

1 tbsp. orange rind, grated
2 egg whites
3 bananas
1 cup vegetable oil
Confectioners' sugar

Mix the egg yolks, milk, and butter. Sift the dry ingredients together and blend with the milk mixture. Add the Grand Marnier and orange rind. Refrigerate the batter for 2 hours. Beat the egg whites until they hold stiff peaks. Blend into the fritter batter. Slice the bananas in half lengthwise, and then slice each half crosswise into 3 pieces. Heat the vegetable oil in a large skillet. Dip the banana pieces into the batter and fry until golden brown on both sides. Dust with confectioners' sugar and serve immediately. For a perfect Southern breakfast, serve the fritters with chopped pecans as a garnish and honey maple syrup. Serves 6–8

EVE'S TEMPTATION

1 1/2 cups flour
2 tsp. baking powder
1/2 tsp. salt
1/2 cup sugar
1 egg
1/2 cup milk
1/2 cup butter, melted
3 apples, peeled and sliced
Cinnamon and sugar

Sift together flour, baking powder, salt, and sugar. Beat the egg. Add milk and butter. Stir gently into flour mixture. Pour into pan. Pat flat. Peel and slice apples. Set into batter, sharp edge down. Sprinkle apples with cinnamon and sugar. Bake at 350 degrees for 35 minutes.

RUSSIAN CREAM

1 oz. pkg. of gelatin	1 tsp. vanilla
1/2 cup water	1 pint sour cream
1/2 pint heavy cream	1 pint rasberries
1/2 cup sugar	

Heat cream and sugar in top of a double-boiler until lukewarm. Soak gelatin in 1/2 cup of water to dissolve. Add to the cream and sugar in the double boiler. Once the gelatin is completely dissolved, remove from the heat and cool to thicken. Fold in sour cream and vanilla. Pour into small molds until solid. Turn molds out onto dessert plates and top with raspberries. Serves 6–8

Savor THE SUNSETS
DESSERTS AND SWEETS

CHOCOLATE AMARETTO MOUSSE

6 oz. semi-sweet chocolate
5 egg yolks
1 1/2 tbsp. water
3 tbsp. Amaretto
1 1/2 cups heavy cream
1 1/2 tbsp. sugar
4 egg whites
3 tsp. sugar

Melt chocolate in a double boiler and remove from heat. In a metal bowl, whisk egg yolks, water, and Amaretto over boiling water until thickened like a sauce. Be careful not to scramble eggs. Whip cream and 1-1/2 tablespoons sugar until stiff. Whip egg whites and 3 tablespoons sugar until stiff peaks form. Fold chocolate into yolk mixture, then fold the whipped cream and the egg whites into the yolk mixture. Be careful not to over mix. Spoon or use pastry bay to fill glasses. Chill. Serves 8

MOLTEN CHOCOLATE CAKE

5 oz. bittersweet chocolate, chopped (not unsweetened)
10 tbsp. butter, unsalted
3 eggs, large
3 egg yolks, large
1 1/2 cup confectioners' sugar
1/2 tbsp. flour

Preheat oven to 450 degrees. Butter 6 (3/4-cup) oven-proof ramekins or custard cups. Stir chocolate and butter in a medium saucepan over low heat until melted and smooth. Cool slightly. Whisk eggs and yolks in a large bowl to blend. Whisk in sugar, then chocolate mixture and flour. Pour batter evenly into dishes. (Can be made 1 day ahead, covered and chilled.)

Bake cakes until sides are set, but center is soft and runny, about 11 minutes or up to 14 minutes if batter has been refrigerated. Run a knife around cakes to loosen, immediately invert cakes onto plates. Serve with vanilla ice cream. Serves 6

PEANUT BUTTER TEMPTATIONS

1/2 cup butter
1/2 cup peanut butter
1/2 cup sugar
1/2 cup brown sugar
1 egg
1/2 tsp. vanilla
1 1/4 cups flour
3/4 tsp. baking soda
1/2 tsp. salt
48 mini Reese's cups
Mini muffin pans
Mini muffin papers

Preheat oven to 350 degrees. Line muffin pans with papers. Cream first 6 ingredients. Stir in flour, soda, and salt. Bake for 12 minutes. While baking, unwrap Reese's cups. Remove trays from oven and press one mini Reese's cup into each cookie. Cool in pan.

PECAN PIE BARS

1 1/4 cups flour
3 tbsp. brown sugar
1/2 cup butter or margarine
2 eggs
1/2 cup brown sugar
1/2 cup light corn syrup
2 tbsp. butter, melted
1 tsp. vanilla
3/4 cup pecans, chopped

Preheat oven to 350 degrees. In a large bowl, stir flour and 3 tablespoons brown sugar together. Using a pastry blender, cut 1/2 cup butter in until crumbly. Pat crumb mixture into the bottom of a 10x10-inch pan. Bake for 20 minutes.

In a medium bowl, beat eggs with a fork. Stir in 1/2 cup brown sugar, corn syrup, 2 tablespoons melted butter, and vanilla. Stir in pecans. Spread onto baked crust. Bake for 20–25 minutes, until filling is set. Cool. Cut into bars.

PUMPKIN ROLL WITH CREAM CHEESE FROSTING

3 eggs, well beaten
1 cup sugar
2/3 cup pumpkin, or squash
1 tbsp. lemon juice
3/4 cup flour
1 cup walnuts, chopped
1 tsp. baking powder
2 tsp. cinnamon
1/2 tsp. each ginger, nutmeg, pumpkin pie spice, salt

FROSTING:
2 (8-oz.) pkgs. cream cheese, softened
1/2 cup butter, softened
2 cups confectioners' sugar
1 tsp. vanilla

Preheat oven to 350 degrees. Grease and flour a jelly roll pan. Whip eggs until thick and foamy (about 5 minutes). Add sugar gradually. Fold in pumpkin and lemon juice. Sift together dry ingredients, fold into wet mixture, and mix until smooth. Pour into prepared pan. Sprinkle with nuts. Bake for about 10 minutes. Turn out onto a dish towel coated with confectioners' sugar. Cool completely.

To make the frosting, cream the cream cheese and butter until smooth. Add confectioners' sugar and vanilla. Mix well. Frost cake. Roll up jelly-roll style. Wrap firmly in plastic wrap. Refrigerate to firm up.

Savor THE SUNSETS
DESSERTS AND SWEETS

FAVORITE TAR ROOF CAKE

2 cups sugar
1 tbsp. Crisco
4 eggs, separated
1 tsp. vanilla
1/2 tsp. almond extract
2 2/3 cups flour
2 tsp. baking powder
1/2 tsp. salt
1 cup milk
1/4 tsp. salt

FROSTING:
2 tbsp. water
4 1/2 cups granulated sugar
2 1/3 cups sifted confectioners' sugar
1 egg
2/3 cup Crisco
1 tsp. vanilla
2 to 3 squares Baker's unsweetened chocolate

Sift confectioners' sugar. Beat the Crisco until soft and gradually add the sugar. Blend until light and creamy. Beat in egg yolks, one at a time. Add the vanilla and almond extracts. Sift the flour. Resift adding the baking powder and salt. Add sifted ingredients to the Crisco mixture in three parts, alternately with thirds of milk. Beat batter until smooth after each addition. Whip the egg whites until stiff, but not dry, and add salt. Fold lightly into the batter. Bake in a greased 8x12-inch pan at 350 degrees for about 45 minutes.

To make the frosting, mix together the egg and sifted confectioners' sugar. Boil the water and granulated sugar together for a few minutes. Blend the syrup with the egg and sugar. Add the Crisco and vanilla. Beat with an electric mixer until creamy, 3–4 minutes. Spread on cooled cake. Melt the chocolate squares. Spread over cake.

Savor THE SUNSETS
DESSERTS AND SWEETS

DOWNYFLAKE SCOTCH IRISH CAKE

by Julie Reinemo, formerly of the Downyflake

1 1/4 cups boiling water
1/4 cup butter
1 cup oatmeal
1 cup sugar
1 cup brown sugar
2 eggs
1 1/2 cups flour
1/2 tsp. salt
1 tsp. baking soda
1 tsp. vanilla

TOPPING:
6 tsp. butter
2 tsp. water
1/2 cup brown sugar
1 cup coconut
1/2 tsp. vanilla
1 cup chopped walnuts

Combine butter, oatmeal, and water. Set aside for 5 minutes. Add sugars and eggs. Beat well. Sift flour, salt, and soda. Mix thoroughly with sugar mixture. Add vanilla and mix well. Grease and flour 10x10-inch pan. Pour in prepared pan and bake at 350 degrees for about 40 minutes.

To make the topping, heat all topping ingredients to a boil. Turn down and stir for about a minute to cook. Spread on cooked cake. Broil topping just until it starts to brown. If you like more of the topping, it can be doubled for one cake.

MARBLED BROWNIES

1 pkg. Duncan Hines brownie mix
1 (8-oz.) pkg. cream cheese, softened
5 tbsp. butter or margarine
1/3 cup sugar
5 eggs (total)
2 tbsp. flour
1 tsp. vanilla

Preheat oven to 350 degrees. Spray a 10x10-inch pan with cooking spray. In a medium bowl, beat the cream cheese and butter. Add the sugar, 2 eggs, flour, and vanilla, beat until smooth. Set aside.

Mix brownies, per package directions. Pour 2/3 of batter into sprayed pan. Pour cream cheese mixture on top of brownie batter. Spoon the remaining brownie batter here and there, on top of cream cheese layer. Pull a knife through top of batter in wide curves to create a swirled appearance. Bake for 35–40 minutes, or until top starts to brown and get large air holes. Cool on wire rack.

When ready to serve, cut into squares with a plastic knife. These are best if refrigerated.

INDIVIDUAL BERRY TARTS WITH LEMON

by Lee Sylva, Innkeeper, Martin's Guest House

8 to 10 (4-inch) tart pans

SWEET COOKIE TART CRUST:

8 tbsp. unsalted butter, cold, cut into cubes	1/8 tsp. salt
1/4 cup sugar	1 large egg yolk
1 1/2 cups all-purpose flour	2 tbsp. heavy cream

In a food processor fitted with a metal blade, pulse butter and sugar for 15 minutes or until sugar disappears. Add flour and salt and pulse 15 times or until butter is the size of small peas. In a small bowl, stir together the egg yolk and heavy cream. Add to the mixture and pulse until incorporated. The dough will be crumbly. Pour into a Ziploc bag and knead until it becomes one smooth piece. Flatten into a 6-inch disc. Wrap and refrigerate for 30 minutes.

Preheat oven to 425 degrees. Roll dough between lightly floured sheets of plastic wrap to a circle 1/16-inch thick. Remove the top piece of the plastic and cut a 5 1/2-inch circle for each tart pan. Line each pan with the dough, then line again with rounds of parchment paper or small coffee filters. Fill the parchment with dried beans or rice, for weights, making sure they are pushed well up on the sides.

Bake at 425 degrees for 5 minutes, then lower the temperature to 350 degrees. Lift out the weights and paper and continue baking another 2 to 3 minutes. If the centers rise while baking, press them down with your fingertips. The tart shells should be lightly browned. Remove, cool and un-mold.

RICOTTA CREAM:

2 cups whole-milk ricotta cheese	3 tbsp. Amaretto or Grand Marnier
1/4 cup powdered sugar	Fresh berries

Drain any excess liquid off the ricotta cheese. Purée in a food processor until smooth. Add the powdered sugar and liquor. Blend well. Just before serving, spoon a layer of ricotta mixture into the tart shells. Arrange fresh berries on top.

Savor THE SUNSETS
DESSERTS AND SWEETS

LEMON LUSH

1 cup flour
1/2 cup margarine
2 tbsp. sugar
8 oz. cream cheese
1 1/2 cup Cool Whip
1 cup confectioners' sugar
3 pkgs. instant lemon pudding mix
3 1/2 cups milk
1 1/2 tbsp. Cool Whip

Mix the flour, margarine and sugar to form dough. It's like a pie crust. Press into the bottom of an ungreased 9x13-inch pan. Bake at 350 degrees for 15–20 minutes. Let cool. Mix the cream cheese, Cool Whip and confectioners' sugar together until smooth and creamy. Spread this over the cooled crust.

Mix the 3 packages of lemon pudding with the milk. Beat until thick. Spread over the cream cheese layer. Cover with the remaining Cool Whip. Refrigerate until ready to serve. Cut into 24 pieces.

HUMMINGBIRD CAKE

3 cups flour
1 tsp. baking soda
1 tsp. salt
1 tsp. cinnamon
2 cups sugar
1 1/2 cups vegetable oil
3 large eggs, lightly beaten
1 (8-oz.) can crushed pineapple with liquid
2 cups mashed bananas (about 5 bananas)
3 1/2 oz. flaked coconut
1 1/2 tsp. vanilla extract

Preheat oven to 350 degrees. Butter and flour a 10-inch tube pan with removeable bottom. In a large bowl, sift together the first 4 ingredients. Add sugar and combine well.

In another bowl, combine next 4 ingredients. Add to dry ingredients and stir until just combined. Stir in the coconut and vanilla.

Pour into a prepared pan. Bake 1 hour 10 minutes to 1 hour 20 minutes or until tester comes out clean. Cool cake on a wire rack for 15 minutes. Remove sides of pan and cool cake completely on tube on rack. Run knife around bottom of pan and tube. Invert cake on plate.

ZUCCHINI CHOCOLATE CAKE

1/2 cup unsalted butter
1/2 cup vegetable oil
1 3/4 cups sugar
2 eggs
1 tsp. vanilla
1/2 cup sour milk, (use 1 tsp. of lemon to sour milk)
1/4 cup chocolate chips, set aside
2 1/2 cups flour
4 tsp. baking powder
1 tsp. baking soda
4 tbsp. cocoa
1/2 tsp. cinnamon
1/2 tsp. cloves
Firm flesh of one large zucchini squash,
        with seeds and pulp removed, finely diced

Cream butter, oil, and sugar. Mix in eggs, vanilla, and sour milk. Mix together the dry ingredients, then add to the creamed mixture. Beat well. Stir in the zucchini and mix well.

Spoon into a 9x12-inch greased and floured pan. Sprinkle top with chocolate chips. Bake at 325 degrees for 45 to 55 minutes, until toothpick comes out clean and dry.

TIRAMISU

4 eggs
1/4 cup brandy
1 lb. mascarpone cheese
1/2 cup sugar

1 pkg. dry ladyfingers
1/2 cup espresso or strong coffee
2 oz. semi-sweet chocolate, grated

Separate the egg yolks into1 large bowl and the egg whites into another large bowl. Add the brandy to the egg yolks and stir until blended. Add the cheese and stir to mix well. Beat the egg whites until soft peaks form. Add the sugar, gradually, beating constantly until stiff peaks form. Add 1/2 of the egg whites to the cheese mixture and blend well. Fold in the remaining egg whites gently.

Dip the ladyfingers quickly into the espresso; do not saturate. Arrange flat side down in a shallow 10-inch round dish. Layer the cheese mixture, 1/2 of the chocolate, and the remaining ladyfingers in the prepared dish. Spread the remaining cheese mixture over the top. Sprinkle with the remaining chocolate. Chill, covered, for at least 8 to 12 hours before serving. Serves 6

Savor THE SUNSETS
DESSERTS AND SWEETS

DOUBLE FROSTED BROWNIES

1 pkg. fudge brownie mix (13x9-inch pan size)
1/2 cup butter or margarine, softened
1 1/2 cup confectioners' sugar
2 tbsp. instant vanilla pudding mix
2 to 3 tbsp. milk
1 (16-oz.) can chocolate fudge frosting

Prepare brownie mix according to package directions. Spread the batter into a greased 13x9x2-inch baking pan. Bake at 350 degrees for 25–30 minutes or until a toothpick inserted 2 inches from side of pan comes out clean. Cool completely on a wire rack.

In a mixing bowl, beat butter, sugar and pudding mix until blended. Add enough milk to achieve spreading consistency. Frost the brownies. Cover and refrigerate for 30 minutes.

Remove from the refrigerator and spread the brownies with fudge frosting. Cut into bars. Store in refrigerator.

If you have enough time, refrigerate before cutting into bars to allow the frosting to harden. Yield: 3 dozen brownies

STRAWBERRIES ROMANOFF

1 1/2 quarts fresh strawberries, cut into halves
2 tbsp. sugar
2 tbsp. Cointreau
1 pint vanilla ice cream, softened
1 cup whipping cream, whipped
1/4 cup lemon juice
2 tbsp. Cointreau

Place the strawberries in a serving bowl. Sprinkle with the sugar and 2 tablespoons Cointreau. Chill, covered, in the refrigerator.

Beat the ice cream in a bowl using a wooden spoon. Fold in the whipped cream, lemon juice, and 2 tablespoons Cointreau. Pour over the strawberries and serve immediately. Serves 4

Savor Nantucket
RECIPE CONTRIBUTORS

Ann Marie Wisiaeko
Barbara Dillon
Barbara Maffei
Bette Gauvin
Betty Marks
Billie Olson
Brian Davis
Bruce Dilts
Carol Barrett
Chef Dante Benatti, *The Atlantic Café*
Chef Eric Widmer, *Palm Springs, CA*
Chef John Hentshel, *Siesta Key, FL*
Chef All Kovalencik, *Company of the Cauldron*
Chef Hector Rivas, *Kitty Murtagh's*
Chef Thomas Proch, *The Club Car*
Cheryl Coffin
Chris Roberts
Christina Craighead
Christopher Bell
Christopher Sylvia
Claire Raneri
Colleen McLaughlin
Constance Murphy
Corky Ranney
David Caron
Denise O'Leary
Donna Horne
Eileen Howard
Elizabeth Flanagan
Ellen McCall
Ellie Huyser
Elsie Niles
Father Paul Caron
Geo. Davis
Inez Scanzo
Jane Bonvini
Janet Coffin
Jean Poupart
Jeannette Killen
Jennifer Frazier
Jennifer Killen
Joan Fisher
Jo-Ann Winn
Joe Amato
John O'Connor
Jorene Whitney
Joy Marks
Judith Amato
Judith Ryan
Judith Wodynski
Julie Reinemo

June Johnson
Kathleen J. Balazs
Kathleen Sayle
Kay Baird
Kay Mack
Kirk Nelson
Laurie Paterson
Lee Rand Burne
Lee Sylva
Leigh Topham
Linda Roberts
Lionel Hart
Lisa Goodwin
Lorraine Light
Marguerite Lewis
Martha Butler
Marti Kopacz
Mary Glowacki
Mary Malavase
Mary R. Thompson
Mary Stanley
Maureen Herman
Melissa Kniskern
Michael Silva
Miki Lovett
Mimi Congdon
Monique Harrington
Nonie Slavitz
Pam Anderson
Pat Riley
Pat Sanginetti
Paul Clarke
Phil Stambaugh
Shirley Souza
Philippa Radin
Rita Moran
Rita Murphy Ring
Robert Burros
Roberta Santos
Rosanne McGuinn
John McGuinn
Ruth Flanagan
Shirley Stehman
Soo Woodley
Susan Lewis
Susan Mack
The Caron Brothers
Valerie Maillow
Veronica Folger
Virginia Jones

Special thanks to the Nantucket Gourmet

Index

Lobster de Jonghe	155
Mussels with Parsley and Garlic	146
North Atlantic Salmon Pasta	174
Polenta-Crusted Swordfish	165
Roast Striped Bass	174
Salmon Croquettes	166
Scallops Italiano	152
Shrimp with Champagne Beurre Blanc	150
Stuffed Baked Bluefish	176

Shrimp

Baked Shrimp in Lemony Garlic Sauce	156
Baked Stuffed Shrimp	156
Company Shrimp	155
Deviled Eggs with Shrimp	24
Orange-Ginger Shrimp Snacks	16
Shrimp and Vegetable Pasta Salad	97
Shrimp with Champagne Beurre Blanc	150
Stuffed Scampi	16

Soups

Carrot Dill Soup	70
Cauliflower Soup	64
Chicken and Wild Rice Soup	66
Chilled Summer Peach Soup	77
Corn Chowder	74
Curried Butternut Squash and Apple Bisque	71
Italian Sausage Soup	66
Kale Soup	69
New England Quahog Chowder	73
Sherried Mushroom Soup	70
The Soup of Tomatoes	64

Veal

Osso Bucco	198
Veal Marsala	201

Vegetables

Baked Carrots	126
String Beans with Corn and Carrots	121
Sweet Pickled Beets	121
Butter Balls for Vegetables	114
Molded Rice w/Spinach and Parmesan Cheese	133
Baked Celery Casserole	132
Braised Leeks	125
Cauliflower Milanese	129
Eggplant Parmigiana	136
Glazed Pearl Onions with Raisins and Almonds	122
Harvest Torta	130
Lima Beans Italian Style	126
Pan-Glazed Parsnips with Sherry	120
Roasted Fall Vegetables	130
Roasted Onions	122
Scalloped Turnip	135
Spinach Provençal	118